YOU CAN RUN BUT YOU CAN'T HIDE

THE LIFE OF JONAH

YOU CAN RUN BUT YOU CAN'T HIDE

THE LIFE OF JONAH

DENIS LYLE

AMBASSADOR

BELFAST, NORTHERN IRELAND
GREENVILLE, SOUTH CAROLINA

You Can Run But You Can't Hide
© Copyright 2004 Denis Lyle

www.denislyle.com

ISBN 1 84030 154 6

Ambassador Publications
a division of
Ambassador Productions Ltd.
Providence House
Ardenlee Street,
Belfast,
BT6 8QJ
Northern Ireland
www.ambassador-productions.com

Emerald House
427 Wade Hampton Blvd.
Greenville
SC 29609, USA
www.emeraldhouse.com

CONTENTS

FOREWORD

It was a few years ago while visiting Northern Ireland that I was invited to preach at the Lurgan Baptist Church for a Sunday evening service. What a blessing it was to arrive and find a full house of believers eager to hear God's Word. It was earlier that afternoon that I first met Pastor Denis Lyle. From the moment he picked me up to take me to the services I felt a kindred spirit and a bond with his heart for the love he has for our Lord and his devotion to the preaching of God's Word. I will always be thankful for God allowing our paths to cross.

It is with great joy that I write just a word as the Foreword of his latest book. The Book of Jonah has long been a favourite of mine and one that is as relevant and needful in our hour as any book in the Bible. As I have studied and preached from the Book of Jonah on different ocasions, I was always disappointed that I could not find more resources in which to turn for insight into the great message of the book. I am grateful that Pastor Lyle has given us a new and fresh tool to better understand and appreciate the Book of Jonah.

Whether you are a preacher of God's Word, a teacher of God's wonderful truth or one who just wants to learn more about Jonah, you will find this book a help. Even more important, it will speak to your heart and bring you closer to the God of Jonah.

Ken D. Trivette, Pastor
Chattanooga, Tennessee, USA

MY NAME IS JONAH

1 Who has not heard of Jonah? Nahum, Obadiah and Habakkuk are hardly names you might find in the latest edition of "Choosing A Name for Your Baby". Ask the man on the street who these men are and you may hear him reply "I haven't a clue. I wouldn't know them if I met them in my soup." To further suggest that these unknown men are three of the twelve Minor Prophets would probably not impress an unacquainted stranger. The Minor Prophets do not rank as familiar heroes in our modern society. Even among professed Christians there is a general ignorance about these twelve preaching prophets whose writings are found in one of the most neglected areas of the Bible.

However, there is one name that does stand out among these ancient worthies, not because of his preaching, but because of his association with a certain Mediterranean fish. We have all heard of Jonah.

Jonah's fraternization with the large fish and subsequent survival after three days in the fish's belly, is one of the most amazing stories from the pages of the Old Testament. However, there is more to Jonah than his encounter with the big fish. Jonah, at his own request, had been tossed from a ship into the Med by some mariners. Conscious that he was smarting from his rebellion against God's will, Jonah invited the sailors to cast him overboard. In more ways than one Jonah felt his life was finished and his ministry was all washed up.

However, even this gross failure on Jonah's part does not reveal the central truth that comes to us from this short Bible book of four chapters. Unlike most of the other prophetic books, Jonah is largely narrative. It does not contain lengthy prophetic messages of comfort or condemnation, but rather it is a record of dramatic and action-packed events. I invite you to invest ten minutes to read these forty-eight verses. You will find that the lessons they teach can affect your life for eternity.

Like all the scriptures, Jonah points to and reflects the coming Messiah. Jonah's experience was a shadow of the Saviour's resurrection and Jesus Christ Himself singled this out, as a truth taught plainly in this prophecy.

The real heart of the story is a message of forgiveness. Mercy and forgiveness pervade this short book. Jonah admitted in his prayer, "I knew that thou art a gracious God, and merciful, slow to anger, and of great kindness, and repentest thee of the evil" (Jonah 4:1).

God is gracious when He gives us what we do not deserve. God is merciful when He spares us from what we do deserve. The pagan mariners experienced God's mercy and forgiveness when they called upon God in midst of a life-threatening storm.

Grace and mercy were accorded to the great city of Nineveh, even though the inhabitants of that city were deserving of judgement.

It was also the mercy and grace of God that spared Jonah from the death he deserved and God's loving kindness provided the repentant prophet with a second chance. Some commentators indicate that Jehovah is "the God of the second chance."

Jonah was not the first servant of God to make this discovery. Abraham, the Father of the faithful, made a diversion to Egypt where he almost caused his wife to become an adulteress. God restored His servant and gave to Abraham a second chance.

Moses, the meekest man that ever lived, disobediently smote the rock twice and broke the tablets of God's law. God did not give Moses what he deserved. A merciful and gracious God gave His law to Moses a second time.

Samson sinned against God and his parents and suffered for his immorality, but God was merciful and gave him a second chance. Peter repeatedly denied his Lord Jesus with oaths and curses and yet the Saviour met Peter on the shore of Galilee after the resurrection and gave him a second chance. I am glad that God does not give up on us when we fail. Jonah disobeyed the Lord, but "the Word of the Lord came unto Jonah the second time" (Jonah 3:1).

The book of Jonah is held in high esteem by the Jews who to this very day still maintain the ancient custom of reading the prophecy on the afternoon of the Day of Atonement (Yom Kippur) to encourage repentance in their nation as happened in Nineveh. Although included among the twelve Minor Prophets, Jonah's prophecy differs from all the others in that it does not give any verbal prophetic predictions. The book is an autobiography of the prophet himself. Hosea's prophecy is also biographical in part, but God gives verbal messages through His servant.

The prophecy of Jonah consists of four chapters and forty-eight verses and is worthy of inclusion in a real life drama series. Here was a man who was put overboard in the midst of a storm. He was swallowed by a fish which, after three days in its belly, delivered him safely on the shore. He must have been such an awesome sight as he entered into the great city. When he preached he probably saw over a million sinners repent. The aftermath of his success resulted in personal melancholy and discouragement. What a story!

Of all the supernatural happenings in the Bible, few have received so much ridicule and derision as the story of Jonah. Some scholars would relegate the story of Jonah to the regions of myth and fable only to be told to children. Not only does history document occasions when people were swallowed by large sea creatures and surviving to tell the story, but also there are ample records of large populations repenting and turning to God as happened in Nineveh.

Some Christians might say, "What does it matter?" It matters a lot. The Psalmist posed a question many years ago, "If the foundations be destroyed what can the righteous do?" The Bible's account about Jonah is not incidental to our faith. It is fundamental.

As a pastor I have no difficulty in accepting the historicity of Jonah and the authenticity of the scriptural record. The historical section of the Old Testament refers to Jonah as a real person and a genuine prophet. According to 2 Kings 14:25 it was Jonah who predicted the restoration of the land of Israel to its ancient boundaries during the reign of King Jeroboam II 793-758 BC.

Furthermore, in addition to this historical reference in the Old Testament, we also have the words of the Lord Jesus in the New Testament when He said, "For as Jonas was three days and three nights in the whale's belly so shall the Son of Man be three days and three nights in the heart of the earth" (Matthew 12:40).

To deny the historicity of Jonah in the Old Testament is to call into question the integrity of the Saviour in the New Testament for He publicly referred to Jonah on two separate accounts. First, He spoke of Jonah in relation to the demands of the Pharisees for a sign of Christ's Messianic credentials: "Then certain of the scribes and of the Pharisees answered, saying, Master, we would see a sign from thee. But he answered and said unto them, An evil and adulterous generation seeketh after a sign; and there shall no sign be given to it, but the sign of the prophet Jonas: For as Jonas was three days and three nights in the whale's belly; so shall the Son of man be three days and three nights in the heart of the earth" (Matthew 12:38-40).

Again the Saviour repudiated the unbelief of the Pharisees when He said, "The men of Nineveh shall rise in judgement with this generation, and shall condemn it: because they repented at the preaching of Jonas; and, behold, a greater than Jonas is here" (Matthew 12:41).

On the first of these two references to Jonah, Jesus Christ related the ancient prophet to His own resurrection. If Jonah's experience was not historical then to associate it with Christ's resurrection would have been senseless. The Saviour did not lie nor was He mistaken when He said that Jonah was in a fish's belly three days and three nights, nor was Jesus Christ deceived. Jesus Christ is "the Truth." His Word cannot be broken.

Criticisms against the story of Jonah remind me of the young girl in elementary school who was studying about the ocean. The teacher tried to reassure the class, "I don't want any of you to ever be afraid of going into the sea because there are no sea creatures that can swallow you whole."

This little girl raised her hand and said, "I learned in church that a great fish swallowed Jonah whole."

The teacher scoffed at that and said, "That's impossible. It could never happen."

The girl answered, "When I get to heaven I'll ask Jonah myself and find out if it was true".

The teacher asked, "What if Jonah didn't go to heaven?"

To this the girl said, "Then you can ask him."

Our ignorance of the Word of God does not allow us to take from its historicity simply because something is miraculous. Christ said that Jonah was a "sign" pointing to His own death and resurrection. Christ's reference confirms our confidence in the inspiration and inerrancy of the Holy Scriptures.

Perhaps it is for that very reason that Jonah's prophecy is one of the most openly attacked books in the Bible. To undermine the story of Jonah is to undermine the gospel. If the book of Jonah is not true then what confidence can we have in the gospel records? I suspect that the same people who deny the historical authenticity of Jonah, will also deny the authenticity of the resurrection of Jesus Christ.

Never be ashamed to take the same position as the Saviour who not only accepted Jonah as a genuine person, but was also unquestioning about the record of his experience in the belly of the fish.

Of course, if we have no difficulty in accepting the story of creation, the virgin birth of Jesus Christ and our Saviour miraculously feeding more than five thousand people with five small loaves and two fishes, then there should be not trouble in believing the story of Jonah and the great fish.

Although the "*great fish*" is mentioned four times in Jonah's writings and the "*great city*", Nineveh, is named on nine occasions, the real heart of Jonah's prophecy is about the prophet's *great God* who is referred to thirty-eight times. God's love and mercy is the real theme of this book.

Jonah made mention of himself eighteen times in his book, but it must be recognised that if we eliminated God from the prophecy then the story would not make sense. This exciting book records one of the greatest missionary success stories in history. The story of Jonah is about the will of God and how we respond to it, the love of God and how we share it. Never in all the history of Israel or the church was such a monumental work done for God on foreign soil, with a Gentile people in one single day than that which took place in the Assyrian capital.

THE DAY JONAH RECOUNTED

Under the inspiration of the Holy Spirit, Jonah gave us some insights into the times in which he lived which was around 784 - 772 BC.

It was a day of economic prosperity: For forty-one years Israel flourished under the reign of King Jeroboam II, the thirteenth King of Israel, even though he was a godless man. The nation regained lost territory and expanded both its boundaries and influence. "He restored the coast of Israel from the entering of Hamath unto the sea of the plain, according to the word of the LORD God of Israel" (2 Kings 14:25). King Jeroboam II had brought protection, peace and prosperity into every part of Israel.

It was a day of international cruelty: We must always remember that these Old Testament prophets ministered against a background of great world empires. Just as our generation has lived under the shadow of the world's great superpowers and economic blocks so also Jonah ministered in Israel when the super power of that day was Assyria, a nation that was renowned for the brutality it inflicted on the nations it conquered. The capital of the Assyrian Empire was the famed city of Nineveh, which was also known as the "Robber City" because its armies overran other cities and peoples to enrich themselves. It is reputed that Assyrian soldiers treated their captives with the utmost cruelty. They mutilated their bodies often severing hands, feet, and ears while the victim was still alive. Lips were torn away, eyes were gouged out. There was little or no compassion for women and children. They burned children alive and tortured adults by flaying their skin. They then left their prey to die in the scorching sun.

Seventy-five years before Jonah appeared the Assyrian King boasted of his cruelty, "I carried off their spoil and possessions. The heads of their warriors I cut off, and I forced them into a pillar over against their city. Their young men and maidens I burned in the fire and flayed all their chief men who had revolted. I covered the pillar with their skins, some I walled within the pillar, some I impaled upon the pillar or stakes and others I bound to stakes round about the pillar…I cut off the limbs of their officers who had rebelled."

The chronicler of 2 Kings stated the obvious when he wrote; "The Lord saw the affliction of Israel." God sees man's inhumanity to man. The television screen has brought into our living rooms some of the most terrible devastation and cruelty that occurs in various parts of the world. We will never forget the horrendous attacks on the Twin Towers of New York's World Trade Centre in which thousands of innocent people were incinerated or buried alive. The images of massacres in Bosnia and Kosovo still linger with us and our hearts break to see the starving refugee children in Africa and elsewhere. These scenes do not escape the Lord's attention. He is on the throne of the world and one day He will judge the nations as he judged Babylon and Assyria.

It was a day of spiritual idolatry: Besides Jeroboam II's reign introducing economic prosperity and improving national security, his was also an era of moral and spiritual decline as the nation rapidly moved away from God and slid into idolatry. We read, "Jeroboam did that which was evil in the sight of the Lord, he departed not from all the sins of Jeroboam the son of Nebat who made Israel to sin" (2 Kings 14:24).

We might well ask, "How did Jeroboam II make Israel to sin?" The answer is "by blaspheming against Jehovah and giving the glory for Israel's deliverance from Egypt to two golden calves, one of which he set up in Bethel and the other in Dan." Of these calves Jeroboam said, "Behold thy gods O Israel which brought thee out of the land of Egypt" (1 Kings 12:28). Jeroboam I had already initiated idolatry in Israel, but Jeroboam II continued with this blasphemous legacy of usurping God's rightful place in Israel.

In Jeroboam's era economic prosperity ran parallel with spiritual idolatry. Idolatry is still alive and kicking in our day and may be found in the most unsuspecting places. Writing to New Testament saints the apostle John admonished, "Little children keep yourselves from idols." What is an idol? An idol is not necessarily an icon placed in a prominent place before which people bow down. An idol is any possession, place or person we may put before or in place of the Lord.

God demanded an unrivaled first place in Israel's affection and worship. Far be it from me to catalogue what may be an idol in your life, but we are all guilty of idolatry when we allow anything to rob God of His rightful place in our lives.

2 NO ONE AVAILABLE TO ANSWER YOUR CALL

Like all Jews, Jonah hated Assyria, Nineveh, the Ninevites and all things Assyrian. Nothing could have given him greater pleasure than to hear of God's revenge resulting in their destruction. Jonah's hawkish attitude stands in great contrast to his name, which means "dove." Even though he was God's man, there was little semblance of a dove in Jonah when he would rather see judgement fall on Nineveh than Jehovah revive the city. To send Jonah to the despicable Assyrians was unquestionably an act of God's grace. No right-thinking Jew would have conceived such a plan or willingly volunteered to go to Nineveh.

In spite of the prophet's imperfections, God chose this man from the small hamlet of Gath-hepher in Zebulon, three miles northeast of Nazareth to be His messenger of mercy to a Gentile nation. Earlier God sent him His prophet to announce the restoration of the lost territory to King Jeroboam; "He restored the coast of Israel from the entering of Hamath unto the sea of the plain, according to the word of the LORD God of Israel, which he spake by the hand of his servant Jonah, the son of Amittai, the prophet, which was of Gath-hepher (2 Kings 14:25).

Jewish tradition holds Jonah to be the son of the widow of Zarephath whom Elijah raised from the dead (1Kings 17:8-24).

THE DIRECTIVE JONAH RECEIVED

As God's spokesman and mouthpiece, Jonah was a man with a message from God for his time: "Now the word of the Lord came unto Jonah the son of Amittai, saying, Arise, go to Nineveh, that great city, and cry against it; for their wickedness is come up before me" (Jonah 1:1,2). This was an audible and authoritative word of commission directly from God to His servant. Before Jonah could hear God's call or understand God's will he needed to be in God's presence meditating on His Word. It is through His Word that God speaks to us and instructs us. God's Word is always practical and relevant to our lives and responsibilities.

God calls particular people to particular places for particular purposes. In Jonah's case God called him to Nineveh, the formidable and wicked capital of Assyria, to preach against its sin. The blessing that God planned for the great city of Nineveh began to unfold when God spoke His Word to Jonah. This teaches me how important it is that the servant of God be in touch with God. You may never know how much blessing God has planned for others through your ministry.

Sadly, when that direct call came to this servant of the Lord it was met initially with a disobedient response. When God called Jonah, he replied, in effect, "Here am I, but send someone else. I'm on my way to Tarshish."

There is a great contrast between Jonah and the prophet Isaiah. After Isaiah had seen the glory of God and was cleansed from his sin, he overheard God ask, "Whom shall I send and who shall go for us?" Isaiah's spontaneous response was, "Here am I Lord, send me" (Isaiah 6:8).

God's call in our lives is unwelcome at times. Our response to God's call can either be that like that of Isaiah or that of Jonah. God's call to Nineveh was *to preach reconciliation. It was also a call to repentance* and *restitution.* Those were awesome themes for Jonah to preach in a pagan city and Jonah opted out and took the road to Tarshish instead.

The city of Tarshish was famous for its gold and other precious metals. Most archaeologists believe it was in southern Spain. Instead of Jonah heading eight hundred miles east to Nineveh, he embarked on two thousand miles journey in the opposite direction.

Where has God called you to go? There are really only two roads in the Christian life. One is that of obedience which will lead to your Nineveh. The other is the hard road of disobedience which leads to Tarshish. The way to Nineveh is the way to *revival;* the way to Tarshish is the way to *ruin;* one road is in the will of God, the other is disobedience against His will.

This was a personal call. Jonah was at the crossroads. He was a real person who lived in a real town just like you and me, but God called him for a special task. It was for nobody else but Jonah. God identified Jonah. "Now the Word of the Lord came unto Jonah, the son of Amittai" (Jonah 1:1). God treats each one of us as individuals and speaks to us in a very personal and familiar way. On his deathbed, an old 17th century puritan uttered these words; "One thing I have learnt is that God deals familiarly with men." God identified Jonah; "The Word of the Lord came unto Jonah."

Do you feel that you are living in a world that does not care about you and where you have no distinctive? Perhaps you feel isolated and lonely because no one pays a lot of attention to you; they may not even know your name. You are distinctive to God and He knows all about you. God knows your name, where you live, your circumstances and your DNA. God knows every detail of every care you carry and He says, "Fear not: I have redeemed thee, I have called thee by thy name" (Isaiah 43:1). The Lord is interested in you personally, in good times and bad.

God's knowledge and care for us individually is both encouraging and challenging. It is comforting to hear God's voice but it is challenging to discover what He might be asking us to do.

I vividly recall an evening in my home several years ago, when it seemed that God put His hand on my shoulder and called me to preach. God spoke specifically to my heart and from that moment I could not find fulfillment in doing anything else other than obeying His voice. It was comforting to me to discover that God does not call the equipped. He equips the called. Christian, whatever God has asked you to do, don't argue with God. He has a way of getting His man and bringing about His plan.

This was a perplexing call. While it is true that God's call to Jonah was personal, it also was very perplexing. The greatest revival that ever took place happened in a most unlikely place. It did not occur on the bonnie countryside of Scotland as the result of the mighty persuasive preaching of John Knox. Nor did it take place in the dales or hamlets of England under the great revivalists such as Wesley, Whitefield or even the great Spurgeon. It did not happen in turbulent Europe in spite of the great reforming impact of Calvin in Switzerland, Luther in Germany or Savonarola in Italy. The greatest revival in history was not sent to the United States of America, although they also have been blessed over the years with great servants of God such as Jonathan Edwards, Dwight L. Moody, Rueben A. Torrey and Charles Finney.

The greatest revival of all time took place 150 miles Northwest of Baghdad near to the modern city of Mosul. In the vicinity of the city lie the ruins of the ancient Assyrian city of Nineveh. Nearby is a large mound of earth known as "Nebi Yunus." Beneath the mound lie the bones of the evangelist of the revival, the prophet Jonah.

If Nineveh was the most unlikely place, there is no doubt that humanly speaking, Jonah was the most improbable preacher to go to such a city. Undoubtedly Jonah was just as confounded as are many servants of God when He calls them to the most unlikely tasks. They frequently question God, "Why me Lord?" Jonah had a further question that bewildered him, "Why Nineveh Lord?"

Nineveh was a sizable city. Jonah 3:3 informs us that it was a city of "three days journey." It was possibly the largest city in the world at that time. Nineveh incorporated many smaller towns on the suburbs (See Genesis 10:11, 12). It was estimated that the city was fifty miles across. For that reason it took three days to walk across it and had a population in excess of a million residents.

Nineveh was a strong city. It boasted magnificent walls almost eight miles long which enveloped the inner city. The outer suburbs occupied an area of more than 60 square miles.

Nineveh was known to be a very sinful city. God said so when he commissioned Jonah; "Arise, go to Nineveh, that great city, and cry against it; for their wickedness is come up before me" (Jonah 1:2). The sin and pagan depravity of Nineveh was universally known. Nahum the prophet speaking of this Nineveh said, "Upon whom hath not thy wickedness come continually."

Why would God call Jonah to that city? Perhaps we can imagine Jonah praying in his daily quiet time, "Lord, Nineveh is not on my prayer list. It never is included on my preaching tour. Furthermore, Lord, why bother with such a pagan city as Nineveh?" Had God called Jonah to preach in Jerusalem or prophesy in Bethlehem it might have been more acceptable and easier understood. But Nineveh?

How do we respond when Lord calls us to testify in an unlikely place or to an unlovely people? At times we feel that what God asks us to do does not make sense. Just like Jonah, we love the Lord, but there are some things we find hard to do. That was because Jonah was more concerned about Jonah than he was about Jehovah. He certainly was more concerned about Jonah than about Nineveh. Jonah was sure that God loved the Jews more than He loved the Gentiles and found no reason why he should go there.

So often Christians can adopt a smug and prejudiced attitude of "we are the people of God." Perhaps it was that attitude that blinded the disciples to the need of the Samaritans when the Saviour and His followers visited the well at Sychar. God's call to Jonah should rule out any exclusivism or partiality on our part.

How did Jonah respond?

THE DISOBEDIENCE JONAH REVEALED

"But Jonah rose up to flee unto Tarish from the presence of the Lord" (Jonah 1:3). While the sins of the ungodly Assyrians rose up before God, Jonah rose up to flee from God's presence. Sadly, this was not the last time some evangelists or Christian workers have fled from God's presence when God required them to preach and reach the lost. We have been entrusted with the gospel but often, instead of going forward, we often are in retreat. The call to evangelise goes unheeded by many of God's people while the cults promote their damnable literature at every corner of the globe. Is Jonah a picture of you?

Jonah's earlier service had been crowned with faithfulness, freshness and fruitfulness. However, in spite of all his previous usefulness, Jonah did not grow cold and slowly slip out of God's presence. He willfully and deliberately decided to run away from God. Perhaps like Jonah, your past service has been marked by God's blessing, but then God asked you to do something or go somewhere and you resisted His command. You have tried to do a Jonah and fled from God.

What was the cause of Jonah's Disobedience? Nineveh was to the east of Galilee where Jonah lived and Tarshish was as far west as one could go from Jonah's home. Why should God's man run away from God's will? Why should Jonah have taken such and attitude?

Did Jonah flee from God because of the difficulties he faced in preaching in a great city? Nineveh was so large it took three days to travel across the city. How could one person make an impact on the masses of people in this great city? Who would listen him? Would the pagans laugh at an Israeli preacher? It was a difficult mission but there is no indication that he refused to go because of the difficulties.

Was it because of the dangers he feared? Nineveh was the capital of a godless and barbaric regime. The Ninevites were not only enemies of Israel, they were the most cruel and barbaric butchers of that time. In every city they conquered they left a heap of human skulls and pyramids of bones. Brutality was their trademark.

There is something in the human nature that loves revenge and we often think that God should adopt the same attitude. A soldier fighting over in Iraq received a letter from his girlfriend to say she was breaking up with him. In the letter she also asked him to send the picture she had given him when he left the United States because she needed it for her bridal announcement.

The soldier was brokenhearted and told his friends of his terrible situation. His whole platoon got together and brought pictures of their girlfriends, put them in a box and gave them to him. He decided to put her picture in the box with the others and an accompanying note, which read, "I'm sending back your picture. Please remove it and send back the others. For the life of me I can't remember which one you are."

The soldier felt he had got sweet revenge and this is what Jonah had been looking for; revenge against Nineveh instead of revival.

God had already spoken of the wickedness of the Ninevites and the city was a very dangerous place to be - especially if you were an Israelite. Would they harm Jonah? In the prophecy we never find that the Ninevites threatened him. Jonah might have been excused from going to Nineveh if dangers had been the reason, but that was not the reason.

Did Jonah flee because of the despair he felt when he thought of Nineveh and the Assyrians? The very sound of Nineveh and Assyria must have sickened Jonah. He did not want them to be blessed, they didn't deserve it. He had had enough of these cruel pagans and rather than go there or stay where he was, he decided to quit the ministry and get away from it all.

If it wasn't because he was a coward, afraid of the difficulties or despairing of any role in the ministry, then why did Jonah refuse to go to Nineveh? Jonah admitted the real reason for his refusal after the revival in Nineveh; "And he prayed unto the Lord and said, 'I pray Thee, O Lord, was not this my saying, when I was yet in my country? Therefore I fled before unto Tarshish; for I knew that Thou art a gracious God, and merciful, slow to anger and of great kindness, and reprentest Thee of evil" (Jonah.4:2). He knew that God was gracious and was sending him to Nineveh not just to pronounce judgement, but God was sending him so that the people might repent and receive mercy from the Lord.

Jonah had a sneaking suspicion that God might pardon these Assyrians and spare Israel's enemy. That would mean these oppressors would be able to strike at Israel again. Jonah's sense of patriotism for his own country and prejudice against a rival nation made him run from God.

Do you find yourself wanting to run away from God at times? What might prompt disobedience to God in your life? Is it inadequacy? Are you fearful of the consequences of obeying God? There is more reason to fear the consequences of not obeying God's will. Furthermore, when we stand before the Saviour and look with undimmed eye upon His pierced brow and view His nail-scarred hands and feet, we shall be glad we followed Him in all He led us to.

It is interesting that the text says, "He found a ship." Some believers think that just because they "find a ship" it is providential and therefore, must be all right. It is amazing how skillful the devil is in his manipulative powers and subtle ways. Sometimes you will hear one spouse say to another, "We need to separate for a while for I need some space." That nearly always means there is someone else involved and they want to conveniently find means to excuse and justify their behaviour. In other words, they find a "ship going to Tarshish". It can happen to a man who finds himself in financial difficulties because he "found a ship going to Tarshish." Sometimes a young Christian girl marries an unsaved man because the boys just came along, it seemed the right thing to do - she just "found a ship going to Tarshish. The truth is this, any time we want to run away from the will of God, we can be sure that it will be easy to find a ship going in the direction we want it to go. The devil also is sure to be there to make sure the vessel is sailing on time. You are the one who will have to pay the price of disobedience.

What was the consequence of Jonah's disobedience? Instead of travelling five hundred miles North East to Nineveh Jonah conveniently travelled sixty miles Southwest to Joppa and boarded a ship to Tarshish in Southern Spain. Jonah was fleeing from the presence of the Lord. But how could he? Had he not read Psalm 139:9, 10? "If I take the wings of the morning, and dwell on the uttermost parts of the sea; even there shall thy hand lead me, and thy right hand shall hold me." Did Jonah really think he would get away from God?

A rigid college professor was administering final exams to his class. He instructed his class that he would place the test paper upside down on each desk while the students sat straight. Pencils were to be on their desks and their hands facing palm up until all papers were distributed and he gave the signal to begin. Once started, the students had exactly one hour to complete the paper, at which stage the professor would tell them to stop, put down their pencils and turn in their work.

After exactly one hour the professor barked out that the exam was over and commanded everyone to hand in their papers. As the students quietly filed out of the room the professor noticed one student who was still writing. The professor bellowed at him, "Hey, it's time for you to stop."

Ignoring the frantic professor, the student kept on writing. Thirty minutes later the disobedient student finally finished writing. He gathered up his belongings and took his paper to the waiting professor at the front of the classroom. The professor asked, "Didn't you hear me say if you didn't stop when I said to stop I would give you a zero on the test?"

The student answered, "Yes, I heard you but I wasn't finished for I needed more time."

The teacher was outraged at the student's casual attitude and asked, "Young man what's your name?"

The student replied, "You mean you don't know my name?"

The professor was still engaged when he said, "No, of course I don't know your name, there are over four hundred students in this class."

The student said, "Good!" as he lifted up the pile of other test papers and thrust his into the middle and ran out the door.

The point to that story is that God is not an angry professor who does not know who I am or where I am. Jonah thought he could run and hide from God. I don't think he was concerned about the consequences of his separation from God. God knew where he was and Jonah's own sin found him out.

God is omnipresent and, as a prophet, Jonah knew that. Jonah was not fleeing from God's omnipresence, but he was fleeing from God's felt presence.

Jonah's attempt to get away from God took him downhill all the way. He went *down* to Joppa. He went *down* into the ship. He went *down* into the sea. He went down into the fish. The road away from God is always downhill. I don't think Jonah would have denied this. That downward road cost him so much. When he fled from God he lost his communion with God. He lost his vision for souls. He lost his intercessory prayer life. He lost his money for he had paid his fare to Tarshish and never arrived there - he wasted his time however long that was, he lost his testimony before the mariners and almost lost his life.

Significantly the text says, "He paid the fare thereof, and went down" (Jonah 1:3). It was a very expensive lesson. We always pay dearly when we flee from the Lord. David also discovered this to be true and afterwards wrote, "Thou wilt show me the path of life: in thy presence is fullness of joy and at thy right hand there are pleasures for evermore" (Psalm 16:11).

Paul wrote to the erring Galatians, "Be not deceived God is not mocked" (Galatians 6:7). There are many Christians paying the fare for their carnality and rebellion against the will of God. Ask the girl who married the unsaved man. He was lying when he said he would never abandon their marriage. Ask the teenage girls who have fled home. Ask the man whom God called to preach and, instead of going, attempted to head for some distant Tarshish. The most expensive thing a person can do is run from God. It cost Jonah spiritual peace, joy and contentment.

God still calls us today. When God called Jonah he answered in effect, "Here am I, send somebody else." When we read these four chapters we might be taken up with Jonah, the mariners or even the Ninevites. It is not a bad thing to focus on God in this prophecy; however, look for yourself in Jonah's forty-eight verses for there is a little bit of Jonah in all of us.

Have you heard God's call and tried to go in another direction? Be careful; be sure there's a price to be paid. Would you dare say, "Here am I send but send somebody else"? Better to say with Isaiah, "Here am I Lord, send me."

Mine are the hands to do the work
My feet shall run for Thee
My lips shall sound the glorious news
Lord, here am I, send me.

THE GOD OF THE SECOND CHANCE
3
Jonah 1:1-6

English Baptist preacher, Charles Haddon Spurgeon, recalled a boy who had attended school with him and had a very violent temper. When this boy showed an outburst of anger he would invariably throw something to give vent to his frustration. "What struck me forcibly," said Spurgeon, "was not that he got angry, nor that he threw some object when he became angry, but that whenever he was angry there was always something near hand to throw."

You will observe that when Jonah went down to Joppa he conveniently "found a ship." This should not be mistaken for divine providence. Jonah found the ship because he was looking for it. Some believers are prone to think that just because they conveniently find a "ship," everything must be right. The truth is that any time we want to run away from the will of God we can be sure we will be able to find a ship going to some "Tarshish". Satan always provides convenient transportation for those who are trying to run away from the will of God.

Christians should refuse to readily accept all developing events in their daily lives as a providential guide when they fail to take God's Word as a lamp for their feet and a light for their path. Consider Jonah; instead of going east as God commanded he went west. One moment he was preaching to his little congregation in Gath-hepher near the shoreline of Galilee and the next he gathered his savings and was feverishly scanning Joppa's dockland on the Mediterranean coast in the hope that someone might be sailing for Tarshish that very night.

The Holy Spirit records that Jonah "went down" (Jonah 3:5). That was most descriptive of the steps the prophet took. He went down to Joppa, down into the ship, down below the decks. Down, down, down! That is the only direction a Christian takes when he is running away from God. Do you find the will of God to be a bitter medicine that chokes you or do you feel like Christ to whom the will of God was food that satisfies? (John 4:34).

In the Christian life we can follow one of only two roads. One road leads to our Nineveh in the will of God, the other to our Tarshish out of the will of God. The way to Nineveh is the way to revival. The way to Tarshish is the way to wreck and ruin. One is the road of obedience while the other is the hard highway of disobedience to God's will. Jonah was running away from God's will but before long he discovered that he could not run or hide from God (Psalm 139:7-10). Jonah might have persuaded himself that he had escaped without any consequences for his actions. However, before long he discovered that God was at work. The Lord is not indifferent to His wayward servants.

THE DIVINE ACTIVITY

Note the contrast indicated in Jonah 1:3-4; "But Jonah...But the Lord". It sounds like the moves toward checkmate in a gigantic chess game. Every move that Jonah took, God made another move, until Jonah realized that that there was no way he could win against God. As a child of God, Jonah had to accept God's Lordship in his life and, as the children of God, so must we also.

"But Jonah... But the Lord", in this contrast of words we are struck by:

The power of the Sovereign Lord. It is interesting that the text does not say, "There arose a great wind". Rather, we read, "the Lord sent out a great wind" (Jonah 1:4). In Luke 8 we read the Lord made the storm calm, but here in Jonah we note that the Lord makes the calm a storm. The Lord's hand can be clearly recognised. God was no longer speaking to Jonah through His Word. He was speaking to the prophet through His works; the sea, the wind, the rain, the thunder, and even the great fish.

This was no ordinary storm; Jonah 1:11-13 indicates that there was something particularly severe about it. So often we forget that our God is the Sovereign God of nature and consequently His sovereign power fails to feature in our prayers. This was not the case with the early church as we see in Acts 4:24; "They lifted up their voice with one accord and said, Lord, Thou art God, which has made heaven and earth and sea and all that in them is." The Psalmist said that " fire, and hail: snow and vapours: stormy wind (*fulfilling*) His word" (Psalm 148:8).

God is in control of nature and here He hurls a great wind upon the sea. As we read in the New Testament, the wind and water obey the commands of their Creator; "He arose and rebuked the winds and the sea; and there was a great calm"(Matthew 8:26).

It is ironic that everything in the book of Jonah obeys God's will except God's servant. God sent the wind and it obeyed. God sent the fish and it obeyed. God sent the worm and it obeyed. God sent the gourd and it obeyed.

Everything in this book obeys God's will except God's servant. However, before we point a finger of accusation at Jonah we must ask the question if we are moving in the orbit of God's will, or have we left His will and conveniently found a boat to some Tarshish?

What was the purpose of this storm? Surely God sent the storm with a view to restoring Jonah to the place of obedience. " But Jonah rose up... But the Lord sent out a great wind..." Parents can understand how God must have felt for they know what they must do when their children disobey. Loving parents should not ignore their children's disobedience. The Bible teaches, "Whom the Lord loveth, He chasteneth and scourgeth every son He receiveth" (Hebrews

12:6). When a mother says, "I just can't smack my little boy because I love him so much." This mother should understand that the Bible says the absence of correction is not love. God does not exact something from us that is not for the good of the family, and especially the child. The Word of God says, "He that spareth his rod hateth his son, but he that loveth him chasteneth him betimes" (Proverbs 13:24). Likewise, God is too merciful and too loving to let His children drift into open rebellion without disciplining them!

King David confessed, "Before I was afflicted I went astray but now have I kept thy Word...It is good for me that I have been afflicted, that I might learn Thy statutes" (Psalm 119:71). Do you wonder why the storms rage around us? Is your boat rocking? Are you in the midst of a domestic storm? Have you been tossed into a financial or a physical storm? God sometimes sends storms across our way to restore us to the paths of righteousness and obedience.

How did the storm affect the people in the ship? "The ship was like to be broken, then the mariners were afraid, and cried everyman unto his god, and cast forth the wares that were in the ship into the sea, to lighten it of them" (Jonah 1:4-5). Jonah's disobedience involved others. None of us live to ourselves. Disobedience in the life of a Christian always leads to distress sooner or later and so often others are involved. This is a solemn lesson. A believer can either be a blessing or a block to blessing, a stepping-stone or a stumbling block.

This is also illustrated in the disobedience of Achan, the man that stole that which had been "set apart" for God (Joshua 6:18-7:1). One individual in the camp of Israel sinned and the verdict from heaven was not, "Achan hath sinned" but rather, " Israel hath sinned". One man sinned against God and the whole army was defeated as a result. It was exactly the same with King David. When he disobeyed the Lord and numbered the people "the Lord sent a pestilence upon Israel...and there died...seventy thousand men" (2 Samuel 24:10-17). David's disobedience affected others. It was for this reason Paul wrote, "For none of us liveth to himself, and no man dieth to himself" (Romans 14:7). When things go wrong in our lives because of our disobedience it is easy to blame anybody and everybody but ourselves. Our first question should be, "Lord, is it I?"

I heard the story about some kids who played a prank on a man with a moustache. They put a smear of Limburger cheese on his moustache when he was asleep. Limburger cheese has a very potent smell. When the man awoke he said, "This bed smells." He walked into the next room and he said, "This room smells." Then he entered another room and declared, "Why the whole house smells." He stepped outside and he further pronounced, "The whole world smells." He was ignorant of the fact that the real cause was literally under his own nose. So it is easy to allocate blame all around.

THE DEFINITE APATHY

Try to imagine the scene. The wind is howling; the billows heave while helpless sailors cling on for their lives and call out to their pagan gods. These mariners had experienced many storms but this one was so different. Each sailor was crying to the deity he worshipped, seeking by any means to placate the wrath of the deity he had possibly offended. It is not unusual for people to pray when they are in trouble. It was General Douglas McArthur who said, "There are no atheists in the foxholes."

Besides praying, the mariners also took measures to try and avoid disaster and, "Cast forth the wares that were in the ship into the sea, to lighten it of them" (Jonah 1:5). They had a valuable cargo but they threw it into the sea. When death or danger threatens we begin to see material possessions in their true light. In the light of eternity what are material things really worth?

There is another contrast in this incident. Sadly, while the fearful mariners fell on their knees to pray and took measures to avoid a disaster, God's messenger was fast asleep. "Then the mariners...but Jonah...lay and was asleep" (Jonah 1:4-5). The one man on board who knew the true God, could pray and should have been calling on Jehovah, ignored the need of the seamen and the great means of grace.

Perhaps Jonah would not have slept so soundly if he had been able to see through the sides of the ship and caught a glimpse of the large fish that was swimming along the keel of the boat, and keeping progress with its pace and waiting for its Jewish meal.

While there is a contrast between the "praying pagans" and the "sleeping prophet" this contrast can also be found in a family. Often the mother is marked by prayerfulness and the busy husband more characterised by prayerlessness. This contrast can also be reflected in the church where some believers are active and zealous, praying for the work of God and the witness of the church, but there are those whose only contribution to the life of the church is negative. They are quick to murmur, criticize, and complain while sitting on the sidelines "at ease in Zion" (Amos 6:1). The same contrast is encountered in the world where devotees of false and pagan religions reprove and shame Christian indifference and lack of sincerity by their zeal for those religions.

Note the following:

The present-day church is reflected in this incident. Jonah was really no different from a lot of Christians today who are in the same boat. Many are sleeping while the ship is sinking and souls are perishing. The prophet, a man of God, was unconscious of the plight of the mariners above him, indifferent to the need around him and unaware of the fish that was beneath him because he was sleeping.

When we either misplace or lose an article that is dear to us we are left with bad feelings of regret. I recall my first visit to Romania in 1993; we arrived in the city of Timmisora at midnight on a Saturday night. We had left a pastor off in Arad on our way and then we travelled for another hour to Timmisora. It was very late when we arrived at our apartment only to discover we had left a video camera in Arad. That was bad enough, but a friend had sent a large sum of money with us and that had to be presented to a church the next morning. We recovered the camera and the money later but we had a bad night regretting our forgetfulness and feeling our sense of loss.

Jonah left something behind when he fled from God. He had forsaken his obligations. And the shipmaster roused the Galilean prophet with this question, "What meanest thou, O sleeper ? Arise and call upon thy God, if so be that God will think upon us that we perish not" (Jonah 1:6). This is a text for a sleeping church. Today's world is being torn apart by drugs, drink, immorality, apostasy and the menace of nuclear war. All the while, the church sleeps. False religions and wicked philosophies are making giant strides and the church sleeps. Abortion, pornography, crime, sodomy and dreadful diseases threaten mankind and yet the church sleeps. Do we care enough to warn them? Care enough to take the gospel to them? We need to begin to take our obligations seriously.

THE DIRECT INQUIRY

Try to imagine this scene. The brawny fist of the captain reaches forth and hauls Jonah from his bed. " What meanest thou, O sleeper? Arise and call upon thy God, if so be that God will think upon us that we perish not" (Jonah 1:6). The Greek translation of these verses suggests that the captain only found Jonah because he was snoring.

This was an embarrassment to Jonah. Especially since Jonah had already told the mariners that he was fleeing from God; "Then were the men exceedingly afraid, and said unto him, 'Why hast thou done this?' For the men knew that he fled from the presence of the Lord, because he had told them" (Jonah 1:10). Jonah spoke of "His God." His God was the true and living God and Jonah was His servant. What did he mean then by sleeping? I suppose one of the most embarrassing things that can happen a Christian who is cold in heart is to have someone make a prayer request; "I want you to pray for me."

A Christian named Bill confessed his faith in Christ before five hundred men. In response they questioned him, "Bill, do you really believe that every man without Christ is lost and on their way to hell?"

"Yes, I do" Bill replied.

"Bill, do you also believe in the power of prayer? They further questioned.

"Of course I do" Bill boldly answered.

"Then Bill, tell us how much time have you spent in prayer for our lost souls this week?" was their final question.

"None" admitted a shameful Bill.

"What meanest thou?" We might ask from Bill who as a Christian professes to know the Saviour but fails to be concerned for those around him.

This was a chastisement to Jonah. It was a severe reprimand for a Hebrew prophet when a heathen pilot rebuked him; a servant of God, and he was commanded to pray by a heathen captain.

Jonah deserved to be chastened and rebuked for he had failed to bear witness for God. There had been a splendid opportunity to witness for God and prove God, but he spurned it. How different was the apostle Paul? He also had been caught in the teeth of a terrible storm. Instead of sleeping on board, Paul was serving the Lord and witnessing to the lost seafarers (Acts 27:21-25).

Surely it is in times of acute danger and stress that we need to show to the world what the grace of God does for us, what the presence of Christ means to us and how the fellowship of the Holy Spirit is sufficient to keep us in perfect peace.

I say, "Thank God for the storm." God did not have to send the storm. He could have let Jonah persist in his rebellion. He could have cut the prophet off. However, the storm was a sign that God was not finished with Jonah, nor is he finished with us even though we might have messed up in our Christian lives.

God can use the storms to redirect our lives and strengthen our faith in Him.

4 PRACTICE VERSUS PROFESSION
Jonah 1: 1-10

Bizarre things happen all over the world. A man in Mexico City snatched a woman's purse and dashed into a doorway to hide. It turned out to be the door of the local police station where he was questioned and later identified by his victim. Shoplifting in a department store in Rochester, New York, a man picked up an alarm clock and headed for the nearest exit. The clock, concealed under his coat, set off the alarm before he could get out of the store and brought detectives running. A Glasgow pickpocket got a two-month prison sentence after plying his trade on an excursion boat carrying twenty police officers and their wives.

These incidents remind me of a solemn principle running throughout the Word of God - "Be sure your sin will find you out" (Numbers 32:23). Our first parents found this to be true. After Adam and Eve disobeyed the Lord, they attempted to conceal themselves from the Lord among the trees of the garden. Alas, their weak efforts to hide from the eyes of the Lord proved to be totally inadequate. In fear and shame they were forced to face their Creator and confess their sins.

Jacob's sons were convinced that their sin would never be discovered after selling their brother Joseph to the Midianites and lying to their father about his fate. After years of deception and concealment their sin was discovered and they learned that sin always finds us out.

Achan, one of Joshua's soldiers, must have thought that he had done a good job in hiding the garment, gold and several shekels of silver from Jericho even though the Lord had commanded that nothing be taken from the spoil of the city after the walls fell down. He saw, he coveted and took the forbidden spoil, but he was found out. As a result he with his wife and children were stoned to death and their bodies were burned outside the camp. The incident is a testimony to the same truth, "Be sure your sin will find you out."

King David committed adultery after a lustful gaze at a naked woman. He then tried to cover up his tracks by murdering the woman's husband. David tried to cover up his crimes but the faithful prophet Nathan confronted the King with these accusing words, "Thou art the man" (2 Samuel 12:7). David then knew and confessed that his sins had found him out.

I think it was the old war dog, Churchill, who said, "One lesson we learn from history is that we never learn anything from history." It certainly seemed that way for Jonah. Despite the misdemeanours of others in the past, the prophet seemed to snub the lessons of history and began to run from God.

Jonah certainly wasn't living up to the meaning of his name which is "dove,"- a symbol of peace and purity. His father's name was Amittai, which means " faithful or truthful". Faithful is something that Jonah was not. Jonah heard God's voice and made his move in the wrong direction. God made His move and sent the storm which stirred the sea and frightened the sailors, but through it all the servant of God was fast asleep. Jonah was not praying because he could not pray. He was aware of his own disobedience and knew in his heart that God would not hear him. The Psalmist said, "If I regard iniquity in my heart the Lord will not hear me" (Psalm 66:18). Disobedience cuts the nerve of prayer. You may pound on the gates of heaven, but the Lord will not hear while you continue in sin.

Jonah's disobedience had another effect. Jonah lost his identity. When Jonah went up on deck the sailors met him with a barrage of questions; "Then said they unto him, Tell us, we pray thee, for whose cause this evil is upon us; what is thine occupation? and whence comest thou? what is thy country? and of what people art thou?" (Jonah 1:9). The mariners had no idea who Jonah was. Why?

JONAH CONCEALED HIS IDENTITY

During the whole voyage Jonah's identity had been concealed and he had hidden it from the sailors. Unlike the Apostle Paul, Jonah failed to openly declare whose he was and whom he served (Acts 27:23). Right up to this stage he had not taken his stand for the Lord and that's why these sailors barraged him with this series of questions. They inquired from him about his occupation, his country and his people. A major difference between Paul and Jonas was that Paul was not ashamed but Jonah was.

A backslider will frequently conceal his identity. It happened to Peter when he followed the Lord afar off and even denied his Saviour with oaths and curses. Like Peter, Jonah was also found out. When we follow the Saviour and walk in obedience to Him we should never be ashamed of Him on whom our hope of heaven depends.

The mariners resorted to a common practice, "And they said every one to his fellow, Come, and let us cast lots, that we may know for whose cause this evil is upon us. So they cast lots, and the lot fell upon Jonah" (Jonah 1:7). Not only was the casting of lots common amongst pagan nations but in Israel the casting of lots was used as a means of arriving at certain decisions or coming to some conclusions. The scriptures teach, "The lot is cast into the lap but the whole disposing thereof is of the Lord" (Proverbs 16:33).

In Israel the people recognised that in the casting of lots God determined the outcome. It was by lot that Jonathan was discovered to have broken his Father's command (1 Samuel 14:42). The last mention of casting of lots in the Bible was when a successor was sought for Judas Iscariot (Acts 1:26). The casting of lots to discover the will of God never happened again in the scriptures after the day of Pentecost.

To find God's will for our lives we need not cast lots, draw straws or flip coins. Christians should saturate their minds with Holy Scripture and trust the Holy Spirit to guide him. The Lord Jesus said, "If any man will do His will, he shall know of the doctrine, whether it be of God, or whether I speak of myself" (John 7:17). Unfortunately, some people handle the Bible superstitiously almost as if they were casting lots by opening at random verses and looking for a verse to sanction or prohibit their plans or actions. Reading the Word systematically will enable us to discern the will of God and He will direct our ways. Paul admonished the Corinthians because of their lack of discernment, "God is not the author of confusion, but of peace, as in all churches of the saints" (1 Corinthians 14:33).

I heard the story of a man who rose early each morning and opened his Bible at random and then with eyes closed, he placed his finger on the page. At whatever verse his finger pointed to he took as God's message for him that day. One morning his finger fell on Matthew 27:5 where he read, "Judas went and hanged himself." The man was a little startled at this inappropriate verse so he closed his Bile and repeated the action again looking for a better verse. This time his finger pointed to Luke 10:37 which reads, "Go and do thou likewise."

The poor man was annoyed at this but he persisted and opened his Bible haphazardly for the third time at which his eye opened to find his finger pointing to John 13:27, "That thou doest, do quickly." The poor man decided the best way to read the Bible was systematically.

The mariners enquired of a careless prophet. Instead of God's servant asking questions to the pagans about their spiritual welfare, the seafaring Gentiles asked hot and hasty questions of the prophet. In the truest sense Jonah could not have cared less for them or, for that matter, for his calling.

A careless Christian is a dangerous person. Phineas Brezee founded the Church of the Nazarene at the beginning of the 20th century and for a time it was the fastest growing church in the United States. His powerful preaching was attributed to God's anointing on his life and ministry. He lit a fire in the pulpit and the people came to see it burn. Wherever the church happened to be, unconverted people flocked to hear the gospel and most of them were converted. It got to the point where people were afraid to walk through the doors lest they also should come under conviction of their sin. In his final days Phineas Brezee gave the church a message, "Keep the glory down."

We are not sure what sort of ministry Jonah had before God asked him to go to Nineveh but it is obvious that by fleeing from God he had lost the glory, lost his identity, lost any compassion or motivation in God's service.

Jonah concealed his calling and became anonymous among passengers and crew with no particular distinctive. In modern parlance it might be said he was being 'seeker friendly', just identifying with the crowd. Sadly, his identification with the pagans had gone too far with the result that the sailors did not even recognise him to be a man of God. They questioned him as they would a total stranger for obviously that is what he was.

According to James the world and the church were never meant to be friends. He said, "Know ye not that the friendship of the world is enmity with God? whosoever therefore will be a friend of the world is the enemy of God" (James 4:4). The world is waiting to see reality in Christians, something that makes us distinctive for what we believe and to whom we belong.

JONAH FINALLY COMMUNICATED HIS TESTIMONY

Not until he was challenged and confronted by the sailors did Jonah at last admit his true identity, "And he said unto them, I am an Hebrew; and I fear the Lord, the God of heaven, which hath made the sea and the dry land" (Jonah 1:9).

It is interesting what Jonah said in his testimony:

Jonah spoke of God's slighted people. "I am an Hebrew..." There was no greater stigma at that time than being a Hebrew. The first Hebrew was Abraham and the word meant 'one who had passed over'. Since the days of the patriarchs all Hebrews were despised and looked upon as strangers and usurpers in the land. "And there came one that had escaped, and told Abram the Hebrew; for he dwelt in the plain of Mamre the Amorite, brother of Eshcol, and brother of Aner: and these were confederate with Abram" (Genesis 14:13).

The preaching of the gospel is accompanied with a stigma. Not everyone will embrace the message of God's love and Christ's death. It has always been so. Paul wrote, 'But we preach Christ crucified, unto the Jews a stumbling block, and unto the Greeks foolishness" (1 Corinthians 1:23). To those who believe the gospel the message is as a sweet fragrance of eternal life, but the unbeliever can sense his own condemnation in the same message. "To the one we are the savour of death unto death; and to the other the savour of life unto life" (2 Corinthians 2:16). However, God has ordained the preaching of the gospel for His purpose and that will not fail. "So shall my word be that goeth forth out of my mouth: it shall not return unto me void, but it shall accomplish that which I please, and it shall prosper in the thing whereto I sent it" (Isaiah 55:11).

Too many in the church today have been working overtime trying to escape from the stigma of the gospel and avoid its offence. We live in a scientific age when some churchmen have been trying to eliminate any vestige of the supernatural from the Christian faith to make it more palatable to modern man. The church was strongest when its standards were highest, when its doctrines were clearest, when its message was plainest and when its opposition to error was most vigorous.

Jonah spoke of his special relationship with God. Jonah professed, "I fear the Lord" (Jonah 1:9). In reality he was saying, "I fear Jehovah." Earlier on in this chapter we read, "The mariners were afraid, and cried every man unto his god" (Jonah 1:5). The word used for God is Elohim as in Genesis 1:1; "In the beginning God (Elohim) created the heaven and the earth." Elohim refers to God as transcendent, the God of power, the God who is on high. The Hebrews had a special relationship with Elohim and a devout Hebrew would never agree with the mariner's statement, "You pray to your God and I will pray to mine". The Jews recognised that Jehovah was the only true living

God. The Lord said, "Tell ye, and bring them near; yea, let them take counsel together: who hath declared this from ancient time? who hath told it from that time? have not I the Lord? and there is no God else beside me; a just God and a Saviour; there is none beside me" (Isaiah 45:21).

It is for this same reason that Peter said in the New Testament, "Neither is there salvation in any other: for there is none other name under heaven given among men, whereby we must be saved" (Acts 4:12). There is no room for compromise on this cardinal and fundamental truth. What makes the church of Christ so distinctive is that it is founded on Jesus Christ and besides Him there is no other foundation; "For other foundation can no man lay than that is laid, which is Jesus Christ" (1 Corinthians 3:11).

Jonah spoke of His sovereign God. As if Jonah had found his former eloquence as a preacher, he said to the mariners, "I am an Hebrew; and I fear the Lord, the God of heaven, which hath made the sea and the dry land" (Jonah 1:9). Jonah made clear that his God was not some local deity from whose wrath they could escape by fleeing the country over which he ruled. Jonah's God was the Creator of the Universe, the Ruler of the wind and waves.

As a preacher Jonah needed to have this supreme view of God. Daniel never lost sight that God "rules in the army of heaven and among the inhabitants of the earth and none can stay His hand or say unto Him, what doest Thou ?" (Daniel 4:35). We also need to maintain such a view in our lives. This is the God we trust and this is the God we preach. The Psalmist also reminded himself that "This God is our God for ever and ever He will be our guide even unto death" (Psalm 48:14).

JONAH CONFESSED HIS INCONSISTENCY

When Jonah embarrassingly admitted who he was and whom he served the mariners took fright, "Then were the men exceedingly afraid, and said unto him, Why hast thou done this? For the men knew that he fled from the presence of the Lord, because he had told them" (Jonah 1:10). How he lived was obviously different from what he professed. In the previous verse he told them that "he feared the Lord" but immediately afterwards he tells them that he "fled from the Lord." It is always a blot on the testimony of a servant of God when his conduct does not match his creed. In other words, when a Christian is one thing on Sunday in church but his life on the factory floor or in the office on Monday belies all that he professed on Sunday, that is hypocrisy. Jonah was a hypocrite.

This contradictory conduct so shocked these despairing sailors that they beckoned, "Why hast thou done this?" (Jonah 1:10). What did it matter to these pagan seafarers?

Because of Jonah's profession these men were afraid. First of all they feared the storm (Jonah 1:5), but now they feared the Lord. As a matter of fact, we read that the men were 'exceedingly afraid' (Jonah 1:10). Who fears God today? Have you met anyone lately who fears the Lord? It follows, of course, that if we believers do not fear God, why should the world fear Him. Do you really fear God? Do you abstain from everything that displeases Him? Do you do everything that pleases Him? If you fear God you'll want to remember His Son at the breaking of bread, read His Word daily, resort to the throne of grace frequently and reach the lost.

Because of Jonah's practice these men were asking questions about the prophet's behaviour. "Why hast thou done this?" They asked. The people of the world were not slow in seeing the inconsistencies in the prophet. The sailors saw a difference between what Jonah professed and what Jonah practised but could not understand his conduct. If it was true that Jonah feared the Lord then why did he behave in this way? After all, if Jehovah owned the sea and land how did Jonah think he could flee from His Presence? To disobey the Almighty Creator was unthinkable even to ungodly heathens.

Some time ago a young girl was converted in the North of England. The evangelist who pointed her to the Lord said, "I hope you will come to the Young People's Fellowship on Saturday night."

"Oh," she replied, "I am sorry but I have an invitation to a dance."

The evangelist cautioned, "Now, remember that you belong to the Lord so be sure to testify of Him and speak of Him at the dance."

"Oh, yes," she assured him, with all good intentions to tell her dancing friends of her Saviour.

On the following Sunday the same young girl was in the front row of the church, looking a little bit uncertain. After the service was over the evangelist spoke to her and asked, "Well, how did you get on at the dance last night?"

"Well," she said, "I was dancing with my partner when I remembered my promise to speak to my friends about the Saviour and I thought I had to do something about this. So I mustered up courage and looked at the fellow with whom I was dancing and said, 'Excuse me, are you a Christian?"

He looked straight at me and said, 'No. But are you?' I assured him I was," continued the young girl.

Then she said, "I will never forget the next thing he said to me. He said, 'What in God's name are you doing here if you are a Christian?'"

It was the same sort of question the mariners asked of Jonah, "Why hast thou done this?" For the man of God, it was a rebuke from a lost man. It must have been humiliating. It is always discomforting when we lose our testimony among our fellow travellers in life.

The question is not so much, 'Why have you done this?' The more important question is, 'What will you do about it?'

5

YOU ARE NOT YOUR OWN
Jonah 1:1-16

When reading through the book of Jonah two dominant themes become evident; on the one hand, the great truth about the sovereignty of God; on the other, the plain truth about the responsibility of man. To the human mind these two arguments seem to run contrary one to another and have puzzled some of the greatest theologians. When we say that God is sovereign we simply mean that He does what He pleases and He is always pleased with what He does. For example, we read that "the Lord who sent out a great wind into the sea" (Jonah 1:4). As we noted, every move that Jonah made, God made another move, until Jonah saw that there was no way he could win. God's servant Jonah was absolutely responsible for his own actions but he could not frustrate the sovereign God of heaven.

We have already noticed the downward spiral of Jonah's actions. It is always ominous and perilous when a Christian starts going down. Jonah went down to Joppa, he went down into the ship, he went down below the decks, and he went down to sleep. God took him farther down when the prophet ended up in the belly of the great fish. We must ever seek to keep these twin truths in balance; God is always wholly sovereign; man is wholly responsible for his own actions. To stress one of these truths at expense of the other results in an imbalance of thought and an unhealthy view of scripture. Moreover, we should not become frustrated when we cannot reconcile God's sovereignty with man's responsibility. Charles H. Spurgeon said, "They are like parallel railway lines that cannot be brought together in time. They only meet in eternity."

These twin truths are also evident in the wonderful story of Joseph, Jacob's son. His brothers' jealousy of Joseph resulted in them selling him to a caravan of traders which eventually took the injured brother to Egypt (Genesis 37:27-28). After many years had elapsed and Joseph had become Pharaoh's Prime Minister, Joseph met his brothers again. Looking into their eyes he was able to say, "Ye thought evil against me but God meant it unto good" (Genesis 50:20). Beyond and behind the scheming and planning of evil men, the sovereign God was working out His purpose for Joseph and Israel. God can use the most awkward situations to fulfil His purpose. Someone quaintly said, "God can use a crooked stick to draw a straight line."

The Lord was not pleased with Jonah's disobedience, but God used this situation to ultimately glorify His name. It seemed impossible for Jonah to either escape or survive, yet God brought salvation out of the storm. Observe the situation:

THE POWER OF GOD WAS REVEALED

God had sent the storm (Jonah 1:4). Some people have the idea that God is like an old man with a long white beard who is feebly looking down on this planet and simply smiling at his creatures while overlooking their sin.

That is not the biblical view of the character of God. God not only repudiates our disobedience, He is of purer eyes than to look upon sin. To know how serious God is about sin, consider Calvary. When Christ bore our sin on His own body, God did not spare His own Son, but freely delivered Him up for us, judged our sin in Christ that we might be justified. Therefore, if His children live in open rebellion, run away from the will of God, He has His way to pursue them with the storms of His providence. If we fail to hear Him in the storms of life He has other ways of arresting our attention. The heaven Father used a storm to bring Jonah to his senses.

Having said that, we should also be careful not to think that every time there is trouble in our lives God must be angry at us or that God is getting even with us because we have failed Him. That is faulty and flawed thinking. Psalm 103:10 declares, "He hath not dealt with us after our sins, nor rewarded us according to our iniquities." It is not God's way to seek get even with transgressors by sending punishing storms. For Jonah the storm was God's voice to bring him back into the path of obedience. Charles Haddon Spurgeon said, "God never allows His children to sin successfully." Jonah is proof of that. "For whom the Lord loveth he chasteneth, and scourgeth every son whom he receiveth" (Hebrews 12:6).

God sent the storm and spoke through the storm. He was not silent. He was alive and active in pursuing Jonah to fulfill His purpose in Jonah and for Nineveh. He is the God of all power. He sends the "Fire, and hail; snow, and vapours; stormy wind fulfilling his word" (Psalm148).

When the power of God was revealed in the storm the men were concerned. At first these sailors feared the storm, then they feared the Lord; "Then the mariners were afraid, and cried every man unto his god... then the men feared the Lord exceedingly, and offered a sacrifice unto the Lord, and made vows (Jonah 1:5, 16). Sadly there is little fear of God in our society today.

The sailors came to Jonah and said "What shall we do unto thee, that the sea may be calm unto us?" (Jonah 1:11). The mariners had some respect for Jonah. He did not deserve their consideration because he was a runaway prophet. However, they did respect him.

Jonah said to the sailors, "Throw me overboard." They recoiled from the very idea of doing this for they did not want to harm God's prophet. Instead they frantically rowed and vainly tried to outride the storm. Their action reminds me of David's attitude towards King Saul whom he might have slain, "The Lord forbid that I should stretch forth mine hand against the Lord's anointed" (1 Samuel 24:6). I wish we could see that sort of attitude in today's society. There is no genuine fear of God in the world and very little respect for holy things or for the ministry of God's servants. On the contrary, those who seek to please the Lord are often disregarded and denounced by professing Christians.

When God's power was revealed in the midst of the Mediterranean, the men sat up and began to fear the Lord and respect God's servant.

When the power of God was revealed in the storm the messengers were humbled. We should observe that Jonah the prophet got no glory out of this incident. This was a humbling experience. It was never God's intention to share His glory with another, not even His prophet. The Lord declared to Israel, "I am the Lord that is my Name, and my glory I will not give to another" (Isaiah 42:8).

What is the glory of God? The glory of God is simply the manifestation of any or all His attributes, the manifestation of God in the world. The glory of God is essentially who God is. When Isaiah saw the Lord high and lifted up he contemplated the perfections of who God is, His nature, the radiance of His splendour and all His eternal qualities. On earth we pray, "Thine is the kingdom, and the power, and the glory, for ever. Amen" (Matthew 6:13). In heaven they sing, "Thou art worthy, O Lord, to receive glory and honour and power: for thou hast created all things, and for thy pleasure they are and were created" (Revelation 4:11).

When the power of God was revealed in the storm human measures were thwarted. We read that the mariners "rowed hard to bring it to the land ". This literally means, "they dug into the water". Alas, their strenuous actions and good intentions were in vain for all their puny efforts were contrary to the plan of the Almighty God. It is always futile to fight against God. Paul discovered this to be true during his unconverted days for the Lord said he had only been kicking against the pricks (Acts 9:5). It is also a delusive action for a believer to think he can fight against God or run from God.

We also read that while they rowed hard to bring the boat to land, "they could not: for the sea wrought, and was tempestuous against them" (Jonah 1:13). Sometimes we hear Christians say, "Do your best for the Lord." Doing our best for the Lord is commendable but it is a happy day when we discover that the secret of victory and success in our Christian lives is not doing our best for Him but allowing God to work His best through us. Living the Christian life is impossible. It takes the miracle of the new birth to let Christ live His life through us. South African preacher, Andrew Murray, said, "The Christian life is not difficult, it is impossible." We cannot live it. Our only hope in living the Christian life is found in what Paul wrote to the Colossians, "Christ in you, the hope of glory" (Colossians 1:27).

THE PROPHET OF GOD WAS RESIGNED

Jonah had to learn to be submissive to the plan of God. We observe that Jonah recognised God's hand in the circumstances and ceased to flee from his Lord. Rather, he committed himself to the will of God and said, "Take me up, and cast me forth into the sea; so shall the sea be calm unto you: for I know that for my sake this great tempest is upon you" (Jonah 1:12). How could Jonah make such a request? It is not that he was irrational or suicidal? The answer is very simple:

Jonah saw that his life was not his own. When Jonah said, "Cast me forth into the sea," he was effectively saying, "I'm casting myself on the Lord and His mercy." Jonah may have forgotten that his life was not his own, but he came to realise it again. He was fleeing to Tarshish instead of going to Nineveh to preach. The Lord Jesus put it like this, "For whosoever will save his life shall lose it; but whosoever shall lose his life for my sake and the gospel's, the same shall save it" (Mark 8:35). In the context of the prevailing impurity and moral pollution of Corinth, Paul reminded the Corinthians, "Ye are not your own, ye are bought with a price" (1 Corinthians 6:19-20).

The Lord Jesus also had this in mind when He said, "For whosoever shall give you a cup of water to drink in my name, because ye belong to Christ, verily I say unto you, he shall not lose his reward" (Mark 9:41). Our lives should be governed by these four significant words, "Ye belong to Christ."

There is a big difference between ownership and possession. You can buy a house with the intention of living in it, but if its already occupied it may be some time before you actually take possession of the house. That means you can pay the price of ownership, but not be in possession of the property. This finds a parallel in our lives. If you are a Christian you belong to Christ, He owns you, He bought you with precious blood. However, He may not have full possession of you unless you fully yield and surrender to Him.

Stop for a moment and consider the implication of what it means to say, "I am not my own, I have been bought with a price." When selfishness and the self–life tries to compel us to have our own way, we should answer, "I am not my own. It is not my will, but God's will that matters."

Missionary martyr, Jim Elliott surrendered to this truth when he went to Ecuador to seek the savage Aucas and reach them for Christ. He wrote in his diary in 1949, "He is no fool who gives what he cannot keep to gain what he cannot lose." That is why he cried, "God I pray thee, light the idle stick of my life and may I burn for Thee. Consume my life, my God for it is Thine. I seek not a long life but a full one like you Lord Jesus."

On Friday 6th January 1956, Jim Elliott's desire was fulfilled when he took an Auca Indian by the hand. Two days later, on Sunday 8th January 1956, the men for whom Jim Elliot had prayed for six years murdered him and his four colleagues.

Jonah saw that his Lord was not hard. It is true that God chastened Jonah as He does all His children, "For whom the Lord loves He chastens." God loved Jonah and it was for that reason the prophet was chastened. If you are back-slidden in heart God still loves you. That does not excuse or justify your waywardness, but it should encourage you to return to the Lord. The Lord loves us in our failures as well as successes, in defeat as well as victory. If you have made a mess of your Christian life, and are burdened with failure, come back to Him for He still loves you. He loved Jonah enough to track him down, subsequently Jonah got such a glimpse of the power, glory and love of the Lord that he was willing to cast his life into the hands of God's providential care.

When you surrender to God, your cares become His cares; your burdens become His burdens. God will take care of you for He is loving and gracious. Our part is to do the casting. His part is to do the caring, "Casting all your care upon Him for He careth for you" (1 Peter 5:7).

THE PURPOSE OF GOD WAS REALISED

God had a two-fold purpose in the storm He sent. God had more lessons to teach Jonah; through the storm God would convert the sailors. It is amazing how God works. The Lord told Jonah to go to Nineveh, but instead he went in the opposite direction and in Joppa he boarded a boat for Tarshish. In the midst of the voyage the Lord sent out a great wind which caused the a storm, and through this storm and Jonah's disobedience, these men were brought to know the true and living God. No wonder William Cowper wrote:

"God moves in a mysterious way,
 His wonders to perform
 He plants His footsteps in sea
 And rides upon the storm."

The storm resulted in the salvation of the mariners. Notice the process:

They were brought low. "Wherefore they cried unto the Lord, and said, We beseech thee, O Lord, we beseech thee, let us not perish for this man's life, and lay not upon us innocent blood: for thou, O Lord, hast done as it pleased thee" (Jonah 1:14). Previously they had been "calling upon their gods" (Jonah 1:5). Now they cried unto the true and living God.

There was a real change of heart and mind with these pagan mariners. They cried, "let us not perish" because they were praying for the preservation of their own lives. They also prayed, "Lay not upon us innocent blood," thereby asking that they not be responsible for the death of the prophet. In their prayer they yielded in complete submission to the will of God by adding, "For Thou O Lord hast done as it pleased Thee". These seafarers not only feared the Lord, they also called upon the name of the Lord as if they were beggars before Him. It was similar to the cry of the contrite publican in the New Testament, " God be merciful to me a sinner" (Luke 18:13).

They were made nigh. The sailors asked of Jonah, "What shall we do unto thee, that the sea may be calm unto us? for the sea wrought, and was tempestuous" (Jonah 1:11). These repentant sinners now acknowledged the doctrine of substitution for they offered a sacrifice unto the Lord.

I believe that at this point Jonah is a picture of our Lord Jesus Christ. The storm beat on Jonah in the ship because of his sin. Sin must be punished by death and the guilty one must die. These sailors knew that Jonah was voluntarily going down into death in order to save their lives. In a sense they could say, "He gave himself for us, he died that we might live." Jonah was thrown overboard to spare the mariners, but Christ was wounded for our transgressions, He was bruised for our iniquities: the chastisement of our peace was upon Him; and with His stripes we are healed" (Isaiah 53:5).

> *"Was it for sins that I have done*
>   *He suffered on the tree?*
>   *Amazing pity, grace unknown,*
>   *And love beyond degree."*

As Christians we look on our Saviour as our personal substitute.

They were the Lord's forever. These men never were the same again. "Then the men feared the Lord exceedingly, and offered a sacrifice unto the Lord, and made vows" (Jonah 1:16). As far as the mariners were concerned they thought that Jonah had died. The vows they pledged were not taken lightly, but were binding for life. It is as if they said, "Lord when we get back to port, we're going to worship You alone, when we return to our families we are going to tell them about You." By their vows they promised to be followers of the Lord for the rest of their lives.

It is easy to make vows to the Lord when the storms of life are raging. Sadly such vows are frequently forgotten after the storm passes. Perhaps you have been in a storm recently and promised the Lord something, but since the storm ceased and calm returned you have not kept that vow. Were your vows superficial? Like Jonah, these seafaring converts discovered they were no longer their own. They now belonged to the Lord.

Can you pray with Jim Elliot, "Lord may I burn for Thee. Consume my life my God for it is Thine."

6 THE MED'S MOST CRITICIZED FISH
Jonah 1:17

The whaling ship, "*Star of the East*", was sailing off the Falkland Islands in February 1891, when seaman James Bartley was accidentally thrown overboard after the ship struck a whale. The whale was subsequently killed and James Bartley was found still alive in the mammal's stomach. Although emotionally disturbed for a time, he made a full recovery from his ordeal except for the exposed parts of his body which had been bleached by the whale's gastric enzymes.

Sir John Bland-Sutton, a British surgeon, reported that an American seaman on board an American whaler, the "*Marshall Jenkins*", was swallowed by a whale and subsequently disgorged again together with the whale's last meal of cuttlefish.

In the Gulf of Akaba, an Arab was swallowed by a whale and made an amazing escape by cutting his way out of the great fish with a jack-knife. The Scripture Union later interviewed this man.

A giant Sperm Whale is exhibited in the Smithsonian Institute in the American Capital, Washington DC. The whale was captured off Knight's Key, Florida in 1912 and certainly had the capacity to swallow a man. It measured 45 feet long, had a mouth 38 inches wide, and weighed in at 30,000 pounds. A fish discovered in its stomach at the time of capture weighed three quarters of a ton.

History documents numerous stories of men being swallowed by whales and surviving the horror. However, the point of Jonah's story is not so much the great fish, but rather the great God who prepared the fish. Some wag said, "Too much discussion about the great fish leads to a red herring."

I heard about a preacher who was expounding on the prophecy of Jonah to his congregation when several well-meaning parishioners gave him some book clippings which attempted to explain how it was possible for a person to survive for a certain number of days in the belly of a large fish. I ask the same question that preacher asked his parishioners, "Why is it that we always think we have to explain the miraculous?" What happened to Jonah was a miracle. Take the miraculous away from Jonah and you destroy the miraculous of the gospel because the Lord Jesus likened what happened to Jonah to His own death, burial and resurrection.

The Saviour said, "An evil and adulterous generation seeketh after a sign; and there shall no sign be given to it, but the sign of the prophet Jonas: For as Jonas was three days and three nights in the whale's belly; so shall the Son of man be three days and three nights in the heart of the earth. The men of Nineveh shall rise in judgement with this generation, and shall condemn it: because they repented at the preaching of Jonas; and, behold, a greater than Jonas is here" (Matthew 12:39-41). Is it any wonder that the book of Jonah is one of the most openly attacked books of the Bible? If we say that the story of Jonah is fiction, then we must also conclude that the gospel is fictitious also.

Jonah's prophecy is the story of a man who rebelled against God and then was swallowed by a great fish. There is a lot of debate about what sort of fish this was. Was it a whale? After all, a whale breaks the surface every hour to breathe. If it was a whale what kind of whale was it? Was it a Grey Whale, or a Humpback Whale or a Sperm Whale? The latter lives in warmer waters and several found in the Mediterranean have been more than sixty feet long.

The word 'fish' in Jonah 1:17 is a generic term and applies to no particular species of fish. I suppose to be scientifically accurate, we should remember that a whale is not a fish, but a mammal, although such classifications did not exist when the book of Jonah was written. I don't know what kind of fish this was and neither do you. However, of this we can be sure, this has been the most criticised fish in the Mediterranean.

We also know that Jonah's arrival in the belly of the fish was the last rung of the ladder of the prophet's downward slide. Was this the end of Jonah? No! We read, "Now the Lord had prepared a great fish to swallow up Jonah. And Jonah was in the belly of the fish three days and three nights" (Jonah 1:17).

I suggest there are three pictures of the Lord here:

A GRACIOUS GOD PREPARING

Once more the scene shifts from Jonah and the seamen to highlight divine activity. The phrase, "Now the Lord had prepared a great fish…" (Jonah 1:17) can be translated, "Now the Lord appointed, assigned, designated, determined, or ordained a great fish." It did not just happen that this massive creature of the deep was treading water in the storm, waiting with open mouth for the sailors to toss Jonah overboard. It was by God's appointment, divine appointment. Jonah had already testified to his fellow travellers that his God, Jehovah, made both the sea and the dry land, including all that they contain; "And he said unto them, I am an Hebrew; and I fear the Lord, the God of heaven, which hath made the sea and the dry land" (Jonah 1:9). God made everything in the world and is constantly in control. On this occasion the Lord even ordered one of his creatures to serve a disobedient prophet so that Jonah could be used later.

We might be justified in thinking that after all the problems Jonah had caused and had brought upon himself, the sailors and ultimately the Lord, God would have let him go his own way or might have even removed him altogether. That was not to be the case. God had other plans for Jonah, better plans for His servant:

The mercy God showed was exceptional. Goodness and mercy still follow us all the days of our lives. God in His mercy does not give us what we do deserve – He has not dealt with us after our sins.

God, in His goodness and grace, gives us what we do not deserve – salvation through Christ. That is why God did not let Jonah go.

Later Jonah acknowledged God's mercy was the reason, "I fled before unto Tarshish: for I knew that thou art a gracious God, and merciful, slow to anger, and of great kindness, and repentest thee of the evil" (Jonah 4:2). The Lord would have been justified in passing by Jonah and using someone else, but He did not. God never let go of Jonah. Notice how many times God might have finished with Jonah and each occasion is introduced with the word "but", *"But Jonah rose up"* (Jonah 1:3), *"But the Lord sent out a great wind"* (Jonah 1:4), *"But Jonah was... fast asleep"* (Jonah 1:5), *"But the shipmaster came to him"* (Jonah 1:6), *"They cast Jonah forth"* (Jonah 1:15), *" Now the Lord had appointed..."* (Jonah 1:17). At every turn God met Jonah's unfaithfulness with His mercy.

How many times have we thought God might have finished with us, but He would not let us go? Just when we were at the point of despair we found He is always there, He does not forsake His children. He neither gives us up nor lets us down. The Lord stays with us, guides us and protects us through every situation. God used the fish to chasten Jonah and thereby was telling His servant that He had not finished with him yet. The Lord had more work for Jonah to do and was preparing him for future service.

When Martin Luther stood before the Ecclesiastical Council known as the Diet of Worms, he cried, "Here I stand. So help me God. I can do no other." On the night before meeting the ecclesiastical authorities, Luther asked for twenty-four hours to think about what he had written. It might naturally be assumed that during that period Luther was conscious of God's presence, but the opposite was true. Martin Luther went to his room in utter despair. He shut the door and alone he cried, "O my God where are Thou? The devils rage and Thou art not there. O my God art Thou dead?"

Undoubtedly Luther felt so overwhelmed as if some great fish, a whale of doubt or a nasty shark of discouragement, had swallowed him. However, on the next day when Luther stood before the Cardinals and Bishops, they said to him, "Will you reject what you have written in these books?" Luther replied, "I do reject what I have written if you prove to me that what I have written is contrary to the Word of God, but if you cannot, here I stand, I can do no other. God help me. Amen."

From that critical ecclesiastical forum Luther carried to every village, town and city in Germany the message of justification by faith alone, in Jesus Christ alone. From there the fires of the Protestant Reformation spread throughout the whole of Europe and brought about the greatest revival of modern times. God did not give up on the despondent Luther. He had much more for the great Reformer to do.

Perhaps you have come through the despondency of a storm and feel some great fish has swallowed you. You have had a dose of the blues and it seems all is dark where you are just now. Do not despair. The Lord has not finished with you yet. He has lessons to teach you and a work for you to do. "Being confident of this very thing, that he which hath begun a good work in you will perform it until the day of Jesus Christ" (Philippians 1:6).

The means that God used were exceptional. A comparison between Jonah 1:17 and Matthew 12:40 in the King James Version of the scriptures, shows that what is called "a great fish" in the Old Testament is referred to as a "whale" in the New Testament. The Greek word used for whale in Matthew is "ketous". The word really means *"a sea monster"* or *"a great fish"*. It might have been a whale but the sort of fish it was does not really matter. God is the ruler of earth, sea and sky. He commanded an ass to speak to Balaam, a false prophet. See Numbers 22:27-30. Here God commanded this fish to swallow Jonah alive. Subsequently, God's power preserved Jonah so that he was able to pray to his God from the belly of the fish.

God can use anything and anyone to fulfil His sovereign purpose. To chasten Jonah the Lord used a storm, a fish and later He would use a gourd.

A GOOD GOD PRESCRIBING

The Lord knew exactly what to prescribe for Jonah's disobedience. First He used the storm and then the fish. Jonah, the prophet who had been overtaken in a fault, was beginning to feel the chastening hand of God. The belly of the fish was not a happy place to be, but it became a good classroom for this wayward preacher. There is no finer school of learning in the entire world than the place God teaches us the lessons we need. What did Jonah need to learn?

Listen to what Jonah was taught. The very first lesson that Jonah needed to master was that God's commands should not to be taken lightly. The Lord had said to Jonah *"Go"* but Jonah said *"No."* It was as if God answered in response, "Jonah I am sending a storm for you and I have prepared a fish to teach you that God's commands are not to be taken lightly."

Is this a lesson you also need to learn? Do you recognise that your community, the town where you live, is your Nineveh? Do you believe that when the Risen Christ said, *"Go ye into all the world and preach the gospel to every creature"* (Mark 16:16), He meant what He said? God's command and plan for the world is evangelisation. Perhaps some of us are a bit like Jonah and no longer take seriously God's command to "go into all the world". When God says, "Go", we dare not say "No."

William Carey did not say no to God. He had a great concern for the lost. One day at a meeting of Baptist pastors he shared his burden for the lost in India. He said, "It is our duty to take the gospel to the heathen." Immediately, there was resistance among his fellow pastors and the Moderator said to him, "Sit down young man, sit down. When God is pleased to save the heathen He will do it without your aid or mine." Thank God, William Carey did not sit down. He obeyed God and went to India with the gospel. His motto was, "Attempt great things for God, expect great things from God."

Sometimes we pride ourselves in upholding the fundamentals of the faith, but show little concern for the world that is going to hell. What will it take to awaken the church of Jesus Christ to its need to take God commands seriously? It needs to begin with us individually. Are you taking it seriously? There are many other commands to which we need give earnest attention. There is the command to remember the Saviour at His table; the command to be baptised; the command to pray; the command to give unto the Lord as He has prospered us and the command not to unequally yoked with unbelievers.

Look at how Jonah was taught. God has strange ways of teaching His people. Jonah did not learn his greatest lessons in Nineveh or Tarshish, but down at the bottom of the sea, in the belly of a fish. At times when we fail to learn from God's Word, He teaches us through His work. The root of one of the words for suffering in Hebrew means, "to educate". Belfast-born writer, C. S. Lewis, wrote, "God whispers to us in health and prosperity, but being hard of hearing we fail to hear God's voice in both. Whereupon, God turns up the amplifier by means of suffering. Then His voice booms." For Jonah it was the belly of the fish, but God can use financial reverses, career failure, physical illness, domestic problems or even emotional trauma.

God has unusual ways of teaching us life's greatest lessons.

A GREAT GOD PRESERVING

One of the main features about the miracle that happened to Jonah was not that there was a fish large enough to swallow the prophet. It is more that God appointed the fish to be in place, and that Jonah was preserved inside the fish for three days and three nights before being spewed up on dry land.

This miracle creates a problem for the critic. Many people have a problem and cannot accept this story. The same people have no problem accepting that men can create a submarine which is capable of preserving a hundred men alive for six months at the bottom of the ocean. If we accept that mortal man can make these wonderful contraptions why can we not believe that the infinite God of heaven can prepare an animal capable of preserving one man alive?

This miracle reveals the power of God which preserves the Christian. God posed the question to Abraham, "Is anything too hard for the

Lord?" (Genesis 18:14). English preacher, Campbell Morgan, put it well when he said, "Men have been looking so hard at the great fish that they have failed to see the great God." We have a God who engages in miraculous things. This great fish is an object lesson about the mercy and power of God. I like the chorus that says,

> *Got any rivers you think are uncrossable?*
> *Got any mountains you can't tunnel through?*
> *God specialises in things thought impossible*
> *He can do just what no others can do.*

Although we may try to flee from God, yet He never forsakes us. The Lord has promised never to leave us or forsake us. God said to Moses, "Be strong and of a good courage, fear not, nor be afraid of them: for the Lord thy God, He it is that doth go with thee; He will not fail thee, nor forsake thee" (Deuteronomy 31:6). The writer to the Hebrews reminded his readers of that same promise, "He hath said, I will never leave thee, nor forsake thee. So that we may boldly say, The Lord is my helper, and I will not fear what man shall do unto me" (Hebrews 13:5-6).

Maybe you recall a time in your life when you turned away from God and went your own way. Nevertheless, you will not be able to remember a time when God turned away from us. He is the Father of lights and with Him there "is no variableness, neither shadow of turning."

The great God was preserving Jonah in the belly of the fish. Can you imagine a place more horrible, more foul or more depressing? Yet, "Underneath were the everlasting arms of God" (Deuteronomy 33:27).

I wonder is God preserving you in some situation in order that you might learn obedience? God preserves us in d*esperate situations* in order that we might learn from Him. God preserves us in d*aily situations* in order that we live for Him. Peter said, "We are kept by the power of God unto salvation" (1 Peter 1:5). God will yet preserve us in a *dark sphere,* the valley of the shadow of death, in order that we might look upon Him.

Do you find yourself in the belly of a fish asking, "How can I hold on?" Fear not!

Remember Christ's prayers for you. He is at the right hand of the Father making intercession for you. Scottish preacher, Murray McCheyne, said, "If we were in the next room listening to Christ praying for us we would never be discouraged." Jesus prayed for Peter. " I have prayed for thee that thy faith fail not" (Luke 22:32). Just now, at the right hand of the Father, the Saviour is praying that your faith does not fail.

Remember Christ's presence with you. Nothing can ever rob you of the presence of the Lord and there is no place you can flee from Him. "If I take the wings of the morning, and dwell in the uttermost parts of the sea; Even there shall thy hand lead me, and thy right hand shall hold me" (Psalm 139:9-10).

Remember Christ's promise to you. Jesus said *"Neither shall any man pluck you of My hand"* (John 10:28). No matter how dark the situation, no matter how dismal the outlook, we can be confident that not only are we kept in His hand, but also, "our times are in His hand" (Psalm 31:15).

My times are in Thy hand,
Why should I doubt or fear?
My Fathers hand will never cause
His child a needless tear.

After one of his great evangelistic campaigns in Britain, Mr. D. L. Moody sailed for America. Following a few days at sea, the ship's shaft broke and the vessel began to sink. "I was passing," said Moody, "through a new experience. I had thought myself superior to the fear of death. I had often preached on the subject, and urged Christians to realise this victory of faith. During the Civil War, I had been under fire without fear. I was in Chicago during the great cholera epidemic, and went round with the doctors visiting the sick and dying. I said I could go to look after their souls. I remember a case of smallpox where the sufferer's condition was beyond description; yet I went to the bedside of that poor sufferer again and again, with Bible and prayer, for Jesus' sake. In all this I had no fear.

But being on the sinking ship was different. There was no cloud between my soul and my Saviour. I knew my sins had been put away, and if I died there it would only be to wake up in heaven. That was all settled a long time ago. But as my thoughts went out to my loved ones at home - my wife, my children, my friends on both sides of the sea, the schools and all the interests so dear to me - and as I realized that perhaps the next hour would separate me from all these forever, so far as this world was concerned, I confess it almost broke me down. It was the darkest hour of my life."

7 THE PROPHET'S PRAYER
Jonah 2:1-10

The pages of history are replete with heart-warming stories of men and women who seemingly have been down and buried only to have made great comebacks. They all teach us not to quit after failure.

When the great Polish pianist Ignace Paderewski first chose to study the piano, his music teacher told him his hands were much too small to master the keyboard.

When the great Italian tenor Enrico Caruso first applied for vocal instruction, the teacher told him his voice sounded like the wind whistling through the window.

When the great statesman of Victorian England, Benjamin Disraeli, attempted to speak in Parliament for the first time, members hissed him into silence and laughed when he said, "Though I sit down now, the time will come when you will hear of me."

Henry Ford forgot to put a reverse gear in his first car.

Thomas Edison spent two million dollars on an invention which proved to be of little value.

All these prove that it is possible to "fail forward" toward success. Very little comes out right the first time. Failures, repeated failures, are but footprints on the road to achievement.

No one ever descended deeper into a fish's belly politically than Lincoln. He was defeated when he ran for US Congress in 1843. He was defeated a second time when he again was a candidate for Congress in 1848. In 1855 he ran for the US Senate but was defeated yet again. Undeterred, Lincoln was on the vice-presidential ticket in 1856 but again he was defeated. In 1858 he ran for the Senate and was once more defeated. Against all odds he finally became President in 1860 and presided over one of the most tumultuous times in U.S. history. He finally was assassinated but lives on in history as one of the greatest Presidents on the United States of America. The indefatigable Abraham Lincoln is proof that you cannot keep a good man down.

John Bunyan is one of the greatest names in the field of literature. The converted tinker spent thirteen years in a Bedford prison where it would have been easy to give up and say, "What is the use?" Down deep in the isolation of that dungeon Bunyan wrote *"Pilgrims Progress"* which has blessed millions of people through successive generations. His experience also affirms that you cannot keep a good man down.

Jonah's story also lives on in history to show us that you cannot keep God's man down. It is true that he went down, and how? By his own volition he deliberately took three downward strides; he went down to Joppa, he went down into the ship and he went down into the sides of the ship to sleep. That was not the end. God also brought Jonah down three more rungs; God took him down into the sea, engorged him down into the belly of the fish, and finally, Jonah admitted, "I went down to the bottoms of the mountains" (Jonah 2:6). Jonah was down just about as low as he could go.

The Psalmist said, "I was brought low and He saved me" (Psalm 116:6). God takes us down low to condition us so that we may be able to soar to heights where He fulfills His purpose in our lives. The downward experience is to drain us of pride and self-dependence. It was as the prophet hit the very bottom he began to pray and look up. He said, "Yet hast thou brought up my life from corruption" (Jonah 2:6).

After Jonah was brought down to the depths he was brought up again in more ways than one; "And the Lord spake unto the fish, and it vomited out Jonah upon the dry land" (Jonah 2:10). After an unceremonious landing on the beach Jonah, was glad to be free from the fish. He must have wiped the seaweed from his face as he saw the mess he was in. It was then he listened, "The word of the Lord came unto Jonah the second time" (Jonah 3:1).

When Jonah wrote this short biography he obviously did it retrospectively. Looking back he was able to recall the situation and reveal exactly how he really felt. In Jonah chapter two the prophet recollected his experience in the belly of the fish during the three days and three nights he was there. Try to imagine what it must have been like. I can hardly think of a place more hideous or depressing than to be encased in a fish's belly, and yet it was there in that almost unimaginable place that Jonah was motivated to finally pray. This is the first time we read of the prophet's prayers, "Then Jonah prayed..." (Jonah 2:1).

WHEN DID JONAH RETURN TO PRAYER?

The opening word of Jonah chapter two carries great emphasis and significance, "Then Jonah prayed unto the Lord his God out of the fish's belly." When did the prophet pray? When he was in great need, when he was under great stress, it was then he prayed. When Jonah was as low as he could go, then he began to pray.

Jonah prayed when he was under a severe pressure. The second verse of chapter two gives an insight into the great pressure the prophet must have felt; "I cried by reason of mine affliction unto the Lord, and he heard me; out of the belly of hell cried I, and thou heardest my voice" (Jonah 2:2). The word Jonah used for "affliction" comes from a verb meaning "to bind", to restrict or to cramp. How perfectly that describes Jonah's personal situation. He certainly was in a tight spot with his back to the wall of the fish's stomach.

When Jonah fled from the presence of the Lord he did not pray. When the runaway prophet was on the ship he did not pray. While others were frantically praying he was fast asleep. When the captain woke Jonah and urged him to call upon his God there is no record that he did so. However, now under severe pressure of captivity and the threat of possible death in the fish's belly, there ascends from the prophet's soul a prayer which was well-pleasing to God.

Are we not all a little bit like Jonah? Which of us has not tried to manage his own affairs until everything began to go wrong? Then, when we were at wits end with no way to go or no means of escape, we remembered Jehovah. It was then we prayed. Human nature has not changed much since the days of Jonah. Most of us still wait until we are in a "fish's belly" before we call out to the Lord.

Notwithstanding what God has to do to make us pray, we are thankful that we can pray at such times for the Lord is a very present help in all times of trouble. Even when we are under a severe pressure from our own failures the Lord is still near and His ear is ever open to hear our cry. Take encouragement from Jonah who said, "I cried by reason of mine affliction unto the Lord and He heard me" (Jonah 2:2).

The first step in getting out of the fish's belly is to call out to God.

Jonah prayed when he was in a strange place. He prayed out of the belly of the fish. Jonah's language is, "Out of the belly of hell cried I, and thou heardest my voice."(Jonah 2:2). The Hebrew word used here for hell is "*sheol*", the realm of death. The Psalmist spoke of it in relation to the coming Messiah, "Thou wilt not leave my soul in hell; neither wilt thou suffer thine Holy One to see corruption" (Psalm 16:10). Jonah's prayer room was a little different from the church prayer room where we gather to pray or the room where we pray privately. The fish's belly churned God's servant as the creature frolicked through the depths of the sea. It was a smelly, damp, dark and dingy place for a prayer time. It must have been terrifying.

There is no place amiss for prayer. Daniel prayed in his house (Daniel 6:10). Peter prayed on the roof top (Acts 10:9). Lydia prayed by the riverside (Acts 16:13). Paul prayed in prison (Philippians 1:4). The Lord Jesus prayed on the mountain top (Luke 6:12) and Jonah prayed from inside the belly of a great fish.

Exhorting his young colleague in Christian ministry, Paul wrote, "I will that men pray everywhere" (1 Timothy 2:8).

A president of a large company in the USA said to his secretary one morning, "Let no one in to my office to see me until I tell you it is all right." Moments later the chairman of the board arrived and was told by the dutiful secretary that the president was not available because he had an important appointment and could not be disturbed. Despite the secretary's protests, the chairman angrily pushed through the doors of the president's office only to find the president on his knees praying. Tiptoeing out, the embarrassed chairman withdrew in a subdued way and asked the secretary, "Does this happen often?"

The secretary replied, "This is the way he begins every day."

Have you a place where you meet with God? It is glorious to know that we can pray anywhere and in any time of trouble, but don't wait until trouble comes before you pray. Reserve a place and a time for daily prayer in your life.

Jonah prayed when he was of a steadfast persuasion. Please note Jonah's use of the personal pronoun "his" in the first verse of chapter two when referring to his relationship to God, "Then Jonah prayed unto the Lord his God out of the fish's belly" (Jonah 2:1). Even though Jonah had rebelled against God and was in disobedience, yet he still held to his covenant relationship with God. Jonah had strayed a long way from God, but he never got away from the fact that God was his portion and his possession. Jonah knew he belonged to God and God belonged to him. Even though Jonah forsook the Lord, the Lord never forsook Jonah. He was still his God.

In the belly of the fish Jonah prayed with profound penitence instead of fleeing in disobedience. Although his fellowship with the Lord had been broken, his relationship with the Lord remained secure. Some believers who are out of fellowship with God may think they have a broken relationship with Him. Even though you have gone your own way, you have departed from the will of God and been swallowed up into some chastening circumstance, all is not lost. If you really are God's child He is still your heavenly Father. Jonah prayed to the Lord *his* God and so can you.

Why did Jonah not pray before this? I think it was because he was out of the habit of praying. His earlier act of disobedience resulted in Jonah dropping the habit of prayer which was essential for the life and ministry of a prophet. The Psalmist said, "If I regard iniquity in my heart, the Lord will not hear me: But verily God hath heard me; he hath attended to the voice of my prayer. Blessed be God, which hath not turned away my prayer, or his mercy from me" (Psalm 66:18-20). That means if I choose a life of disobedience then when I pray the Lord will not hear me. When God did not hear the disobedient prophet, the rebellious prophet gave up praying. John Bunyan said, "Prayer will make a man cease from sin, or sin will entice a man to cease from prayer." A disobedient life produces a prayerless life.

Have you ceased from the habit of praying daily? If so, is it because of sin in your life? An old Negro spiritual song goes like this, "Every time I feel the Spirit moving in my heart, I'll pray." The emphasis in this song is on feeling. However, although we need to pray when we feel like it, we also need to pray when we don't feel like it. We need to pray until we do feel like praying. If I waited until I felt like praying I would pray very little.

Prayer is one of the most difficult disciplines in the Christian life. Praying is not easy. It is hard work. It is for that reason there are more exhortations and commands given about prayer than any other aspect of the Christian life. Why should this be? I think there are two reasons. First of all, Satan knows the potential of a Christian who habitually prays. God has promised to answer our prayer in unimaginable ways, "Now unto him that is able to do exceeding abundantly above all that we ask or think, according to the power that worketh in us" (Ephesians 3:20).

The second reason why prayer is so difficult is because of the opposition we encounter when we pray. Paul made this clear to the Ephesian Christians when he wrote, "For we wrestle not against flesh and blood, but against principalities, against powers, against the rulers of the darkness of this world, against spiritual wickedness in high places" (Ephesians 6:12). It is for this reason we need to take unto us the whole armour of God, that we may be able to withstand in the evil day, and having done all, to stand (Ephesians 6:13).

I find that once a Christian leaves off from the habit of praying it becomes very difficult to start again. That's why we need a disciplined prayer life. We need to have a regular time for prayer. For me, it is early morning. Do you have a regular time for prayer? If you do, I encourage you to determine that nothing will make you change that scheduled time with God.

WHY DID JONAH RESORT TO PRAYER?

What was the reason for Jonah's prayer? Why did he pray at this time when he had not prayed while he was on the run? I suggest the following reasons:

The adversity God sent moved the lips of Jonah. Down in the belly of the fish Jonah cried, "Thou hadst cast me into the deep all thy billows and waves passed over me" (Jonah 2:3). The prophet recognised God's chastening hand. In retrospect he acknowledged that God sent out the *"great wind"* and appointed the rendezvous with the *"great fish"*. It was the Lord who had sent the adversity and affliction which prompted his lips to move in prayer.

Jonah said, "I cried by reason of mine affliction unto the Lord, and he heard me; out of the belly of hell cried I, and thou heardest my voice" (Jonah 2:2). His distressing situation caused him to call with desperation unto the Lord.

Can you not recall incidents and situations in your life which made you desperate for God to intervene? When nothing else causes us to call on the Lord, adversity has a way of stimulating our lips and bending our knees to seek God in prayer.

Paul admitted that whatever the thorn in his flesh was, it made him seek the Lord. That thorn was a means to an end. After praying three times Paul accepted that God had sent that thorn, "lest I should be exalted above measure" (2 Corinthians 12:7). Whatever that thorn was, it became the means God used to keep Paul humble, teach him to pray, to prove God's grace is sufficient and learn the lesson that when we are weak, then are we strong.

I suggest that the fish had a similar effect on Jonah as that thorn had on Paul. It was affliction that made Jonah pray.

The Psalmist also learned this same painful lesson, "Before I was afflicted I went astray: but now have I kept thy word" (Psalm 119:67). Is it any wonder the Psalmist added, "It is good for me that I have been afflicted; that I might learn thy statutes" (Psalm 119:71).

The ardency Jonah showed moved the heart of God. Jonah not only prayed, but did so with great intensity, "I cried by reason of mine affliction unto the Lord, and he heard me; out of the belly of hell cried I, and thou heardest my voice" (Jonah 2:2).

There are times when prayer can be formal, but then there is praying that is extremely passionate and often accompanied by weeping. One of the maladies of the church in present times is that we are dry-eyed in our prayers. We have lost the passion for God and His work. Some may think that tears are a sign of weakness. Such people are often too proud to cry, but we need to know that God honours tears, "They that sow in tears shall reap in joy" (Psalm 126:5). He keeps all our tears in His bottle and records them in His book, "Thou tellest my wanderings: put thou my tears into thy bottle: are they not in thy book?" (Psalm 56:8). God has many ways of washing our eyes with tears.

Paul was not ashamed to weep for his kinsmen who were lost, "I say the truth in Christ, I lie not, my conscience also bearing me witness in the Holy Ghost, That I have great heaviness and continual sorrow in my heart. For I could wish that myself were accursed from Christ for my brethren, my kinsmen according to the flesh" (Romans 9:1-3).

Scottish minister William Burns, was standing in a Glasgow alley one day looking at the crowds passing by. Tears freely coursed down his face. His mother looked at her son and was very concerned for his welfare. She asked, "William, why those tears?"

He replied, "I am weeping at the sight of multitudes, many of them going through life into death without Christ."

In his book, *"When Iron Gates Yield"*, Geoffrey Bull, who spent years in cruel and debasing captivity under the communists, says, "The spiritual poverty of my life and service suddenly came before me. With tears I broke down and knelt on the dusty floor. I wept my way afresh to Calvary."

Isaiah went to Hezekiah and alerted him with these startling words, "Set thine house in order for thou shalt die and not live" (Isaiah 38:1). It was then that Hezekiah turned his face to the Lord and wept sore and the Word of the Lord came again to Isaiah and said, "Go to Hezekiah, thus saith the Lord, I have heard thy prayer, I have seen thy tears" (Isaiah 38:5).

I find it interesting that tears, genuine brokenness, moved the very heart of God. Martin Luther once said, "We pray chance prayers with a 'take it or leave it' attitude. We offer that which costs us nothing, we haven't even a strong desire."

Does God have to put us in a tight corner in order to make us pray with fervency? The insightful E. M. Bounds wrote, "Our praying needs to be pressed and pursued with an energy that never tires, a persistency which will not be denied and a courage which never fails."

WHAT DID JONAH RECEIVE IN PRAYER?

The greatest incentive to prayer is not our need. It is the promise that God will answer when we call. When Jonah related how he cried unto the Lord by reason of his affliction, he added, "And he heard me; out of the belly of hell cried I, and thou heardest my voice" (Jonah 2:2).

There is no doubt that God hears all prayer. We need to recognise that the Lord responds to our prayers in a several ways. I like to remember God's answers in this way:

Desire: Sometimes the Lord grants the very desire we ask of Him. This was the case with Hannah when she asked for a son, "For this child I prayed; and the Lord hath given me my petition which I asked of him" (1 Samuel 1:27).

Denial: There are times when the Lord refuses to give the thing we ask of Him. When Moses wanted to enter the Promised Land he made his request before God in prayer. God answered by denying his request, "The Lord was wroth with me for your sakes, and would not hear me: and the Lord said unto me, Let it suffice thee; speak no more unto me of this matter" (Deuteronomy 3:26).

Paul also wanted God to remove the painful thorn in his flesh. He said, "For this thing I besought the Lord thrice, that it might depart from me" (2 Corinthians 12:8). We know that God refused this request to Paul. Our God is loving and wise. He never makes mistakes and His refusals are for our good.

Delay: At times the Lord answers by saying, "Not yet." When King David expressed his desire to build a house for the Lord, the intention was very worthy. God approved of the plan, but not at that time, nor would David have the privilege. Solomon would build the temple and not David (2 Samuel 7) who never saw the magnificent edifice.

Perhaps a more familiar illustration of God's delay is found in the story of Bethany when Lazarus died. Mary and Martha did what was right, they called for the Saviour to come. "Therefore His sisters sent unto Him, saying, Lord, behold, he whom thou lovest is sick...When He had heard therefore that he was sick, He abode two days still in the same place where He was" (John 11:3-6). The Lord Jesus delayed His coming so to demonstrate the great power and glory of God in resurrecting Lazarus from the grave. God's timing is always faultless and His purpose always perfect.

Diversion: On occasions God grants the request we make in prayer, but not in our way. Moses had a passion for the glory of God and asked to see God's glory, "He said, I beseech thee, shew me thy glory" (Exodus 33:18). God answered Moses and said, "Thou canst not see my face: for there shall no man see me, and live. And the Lord said, Behold, there is a place by me, and thou shalt stand upon a rock: And it shall come to pass, while my glory passeth by, that I will put thee in a clift of the rock, and will cover thee with my hand while I pass by: And I will take away mine hand, and thou shalt see my back parts: but my face shall not be seen" (Exodus 33:20-23).

God is sovereign, loving and wise. It is best to leave our petitions in His hands to answer our prayers in the way He deems best. It is always for His glory and for our good.

I know not by what methods rare,
But this I know God answers prayer
I know not if the blessings sought
Will come in just the guise I thought
I leave my prayers to Him alone,
Whose will is wiser than my own.

Jonah disobeyed the Lord, he disregarded the Lord, but the Lord not only heard his cry, He responded to his prayer; "And the Lord spake unto the fish, and it vomited out Jonah upon the dry land" (Jonah 2:10).

Jonah discovered the Lord is responsive to those who plead for his mercy. Jonah's affliction made him beg and plead with God who was responsive to his cry. The Lord is still responsive to those who plead for His mercy. God is responsive to sinners who acknowledge their sinfulness. God's ear is always open to the sinner who cries, "God be merciful to me a sinner" (Luke 18:13). The Bible says, "For whosoever shall call Lord shall be saved" (Romans 10:13).

Jonah discovered the Lord is responsive to saints who acknowledge their slackness. When Jonah prayed he needed to repent of his backsliding and rebellion. It is always too late to continue in sin. The apostle John said, "If we say that we have no sin, we deceive ourselves, and the truth is not in us. If we confess our sins, he is faithful and just to forgive us our sins, and to cleanse us from all unrighteousness" (1 John 1:8-9). If you have become indifferent to God's will, you need to confess this disobedience to the Lord.

Jonah discovered that the Lord is responsive to praying in His will. Previously Jonah had been running from the will of God. Now we find him praying according to the will of God. We know this because he said, "I cried and He heard me." We know Jonah was heard because he lived to tell the story.

Again, the apostle John has somewhat to say on this matter, "This is the confidence that we have in Him that if we ask anything according to His will He hears us and if we know that He hears us, whatsoever we ask, we know that we have the petitions that we desired of Him" (1 John 5:14-15).

Perhaps you wonder how we can know that we are praying in the will of God? I think it comes from a holy familiarity with God and His revealed Word. God treats us with familiarity and we should be reverently familiar with Him and His Word. As God's children, the Spirit of adoption in our hearts cries, "Abba, Father" (Galatians 4:6). In Israel to this day "Abba" is the most intimate and loving term by which a child will address its father.

Saints in the early church were so familiar with the will of God that they came before God in prayer and said, "Now, Lord, behold their threatenings: and grant unto Thy servants, that with all boldness they may speak Thy word, by stretching forth Thine hand to heal; and that signs and wonders may be done by the name of Thy holy child Jesus" (Acts 4:29, 30).

While George Mueller of Bristol was on his way to United States the seas were becalmed and the ship came to a standstill because of the dense Atlantic fog. Mueller went to the Captain and said, "I must be in New York on Friday evening to speak."

"Well," said the Captain, "If we don't leave within an hour we're not going to make it."

George Mueller pressed, "I have got to be there and the Lord has given me assurance I will be there."

To this the Captain replied, "I'm sorry sir, but we are not going to make it. This fog will probably last for hours, perhaps days."

Mueller said, "I believe in the God who answers prayer. Do you?"

The Captain hesitated, "Well, I don't know."

Mueller continued, "Do you mind if I pray?"

With the captain's consent George Mueller prayed and the ship's master later reported there was not much to Mueller's prayer. However, when George Mueller had finished praying, he looked at the captain and said, "You don't believe God is going to do it, and I believe He already has."

When the Captain looked out at the sea he discovered the fog had lifted and everything was clear.

George Mueller had a holy familiarity with God and His Word.

William Law said, "He who has learned to pray, has learned the greatest secret of a holy and a happy life."

Perhaps we need to look into the face of our Master and say afresh, "Lord teach me to pray."

8 LESSONS JONAH LEARNED IN THE DARK
Jonah 2:1-10

Jonah's prayer in the belly of the fish is quite unique among the great prayers of the Bible in that the prophet did not use one petition that originated with himself. Jonah simply prayed the Word of God, most of which was taken up with a number of quotations from the Psalms. When he opened his prayer with, "I cried by reason of mine affliction unto the Lord and He heard me" (Jonah 2:2), he was quoting Psalm 18:6 which says, " In my distress I called upon the Lord, and cried unto my God, He heard my voice out of His temple." Jonah further prayed, "For Thou hadst cast me into the deep, in the midst of the seas and the floods compassed me about." This is a quotation from Psalm 42:7; "Deep calleth unto deep at the noise of Thy waterspouts, all Thy waves and Thy billows are gone over me." Other parallels to Jonah's prayer are to be found in Psalms 3, 5, 18, 31, 42, 69, 77, 116, and 120.

It is evident that Jonah was a workman that needed not to be ashamed, and knew how to rightly divide "the Word of Truth" (2 Tim. 2:15). He was absolutely saturated with the scriptures and in prayer he was standing on the promises of God and kneeling on the veracity of the scriptures.

This is a lesson all of us need to learn. Paul urged that Christians "be filled with the knowledge of His will in all wisdom and spiritual understanding" (Colossians 1:9). Parents should pray the scriptures over their children. Believers should pray the scriptures over their pastors "that they may open their mouth boldly to make known the mystery of the gospel" (Ephesians 6:19). Reading the Word of God and supplicating at the throne of God go hand in hand. When the apostles were faced with organisational problems in the early church they said, "We will give ourselves continually to prayer and to the ministry of the Word" (Acts 6:4). An examination of the Bible reveals that this principle that unites prayer and the scriptures in ministry are prevalent. We should not separate the Word of God from the throne of God. We do so at our own peril.

While the Word of God gives us enlightenment, it is prayer that gives us enablement. When we read the Word of God, our faith is increased because faith comes by the Word of God. When we pray according to His Word, God answers. Without the Bible prayer has no direction, and without prayer the Bible has no dynamic. God speaks to us through His written Word and we speak to Him through prayer.

William Gurnall, the Puritan preacher of several centuries back, used to say, "When people do not mind what God speaks to them in His Word, God doth as little mind what they say to Him in prayer." When we separate the Word of God from prayer we increase our problems. Jonah did not do that.   In his prayer he stood on the promises of God and prayed from the Holy Scriptures.

Something else Jonah did when he prayed; he shared with us the lessons he had learnt when he was in the belly of the fish for three days and three nights. As we already noted, Jonah wrote this prophecy subsequent to his deliverance and the great revival in Nineveh. He was therefore looking back to show us what he had experienced and learned.

I suggest Jonah learned three simple lessons:

Jonah learned that a disobedient life provokes God. Moses also discovered this to be true when instead of speaking to the rock, he struck the rock with his rod, "Moses lifted up his hand, and with his rod he smote the rock twice: and the water came out abundantly

(Numbers 20:11). As a result Moses was not permitted to enter into the Promised Land.

David also made a similar discovery when, instead of going with the men to war, he stayed at home in the palace. From the palace he indulged in immoral desires when he continued looking at Bathsheba, lusting for her and then lying with her. The outcome was disastrous. What began with lust led to adultery, murder, rebellion in his family and finally to division in his home. All of this is told for us in 2 Samuel 12.

It was Jonah's disobedience that led to the prophet spending three days and three nights in the belly of the fish. Jonah learned that when we sin it affects God's witness in the world and our fellowship with Him.

Jonah admitted his error when he said, "They that observe lying vanities forsake their own mercy" (Jonah 2:8). The Amplified Bible translates it this way *"Those who pay regard to false, useless and worthless idols forsake their own source of mercy and loving kindness."* Jonah had bowed to one of the worst of all pagan idols - *SELF.*

The lessons Jonah learned did not excuse his sin. Jonah learned some tremendous lessons in the belly of the fish.

Jonah learned that God's commands are not to be taken lightly. It was a hard lesson, but in retrospection Jonah learned that the way of the transgressor is hard; after all, it landed him in the fish's belly, "And Jonah was in the belly of the fish three days and three nights" (Jonah 1:17).

Jonah also learned that those who live in disobedience do not magnify God's mercy. Jonah refused to accept that God could or would be merciful to Assyria, the enemies of Israel. In doing so he failed to see his own need for God's mercy. He recognised he had turned his back on the merciful God of heaven, "They that observe lying vanities forsake their own mercy" (Jonah 2:8).

Jonah learned that God wants our gratitude even though we are not saved by thanksgiving. There is little gratitude in a hard heart. At first

Jonah had forgotten to be thankful. Ingratitude is one of the marks of depravity indicated by Paul, "When they knew God, they glorified him not as God, neither were thankful; but became vain in their imaginations, and their foolish heart was darkened" (Romans 1:21). How foolish Jonah had become to ignore the goodness of God. When he repented he prayed out of a grateful heart, "I will sacrifice unto thee with the voice of thanksgiving; I will pay that that I have vowed" (Jonah 2:9).

Jonah learned that salvation was out of his hands, it belonged to God. It was futile of Jonah to imagine he might know better than God did, or could devise a better plan than God's plan. Now he confessed that "salvation is of the Lord" (Jonah 2:9).

Because Jonah benefited from his time in the belly of the fish we might be tempted to think that his disobedience was justified. Dr R. T. Kendal, lately of Westminster Chapel in London, makes an important observation in his book on Jonah. He says that Romans 8:28 is often misunderstood and misinterpreted. The verse says, "And we know that all things work together for good to them that love God, to them who are the called according to his purpose."

Dr Kendall points out that just because something has been *made right* does not necessarily mean it *was right.* David committed adultery with Bathsheba and had Uriah her husband murdered to cover his sin. What David did was neither right nor could it be justified. However, not only David's name is mentioned in the genealogy of Jesus Christ, but the genealogy also includes this statement, "And Jesse begat David the king and David the king begat Solomon of her that had been the wife of Urias" (Matthew 1:6). What David did was wrong, criminal and immoral. However, God wisely overruled David's failure to work out His purpose. You might be tempted to think that because God made it all work out for good, therefore it was right. No! Thank God, though David's acts were wrong, they can be made right, but that does not mean they were right. David reaped what he sowed. His heart was broken when Absalom rebelled against him and subsequently lost his life. Besides,

David's daughter was abused by her own family and there followed a series of other grave tragedies in David's family.

Jonah profited from his time in the belly of the fish, but that did not excuse his sin. In effect, Jonah afterwards said, "It was not worth it." God's waves and breakers threatened to swallow him. We cannot play fast and loose with God's moral law or His will for our lives. Furthermore, those who do will make the same discovery as Jonah; it is not worth it for you will only reap what you sow.

Jonah learned that the life he was living did not exalt his Sovereign. The prophet freely confessed, "All that I did, did not exalt the Lord." Jonah has been called an antinomian because he had a taste of God's mercy, but concluded that the way he lived did not matter. God had said to Jonah, "Go to Nineveh," but Jonah defied God, left his home and thought he could flee many miles from the presence of the Lord he professed to serve. He has learnt a bitter lesson and now there is a change of attitude. Revolt has been replaced by repentance, "I cried by reason of mine affliction unto the Lord, and he heard me; out of the belly of hell cried I, and thou heardest my voice. For thou hadst cast me into the deep, in the midst of the seas; and the floods compassed me about: all thy billows and thy waves passed over me. Then I said, I am cast out of thy sight; yet I will look again toward thy holy temple. The waters compassed me about, even to the soul: the depth closed me round about, the weeds were wrapped about my head. I went down to the bottoms of the mountains; the earth with her bars was about me for ever: yet hast thou brought up my life from corruption, O Lord my God. When my soul fainted within me I remembered the Lord: and my prayer came in unto thee, into thine holy temple" (Jonah 2:2-7).

The voice is that of the prodigal prophet who had returned to his Father with regret and repentance. All prodigals need to return to the Father. Although relationship has not been severed, fellowship needs to be restored and redeployment made for God's work. It is easy to be proud of our well-thought-out theology, but we need to learn obedience. Time spent in disobedience is wasted time.

But for me, 'twas the truth you taught;
To you so clear, to me so dim.
But when you came to me you brought,
A sense of Him.

A DISCIPLINED LIFE PRODUCES FRUIT

Christians were created to be fruitful. The Lord Jesus said, "Ye have not chosen me, but I have chosen you, and ordained you, that ye should go and bring forth fruit, and that your fruit should remain" (John 15:16). However, the Saviour also said that in order to produce plentiful fruit the Heavenly Gardener has to prune the branches, "Every branch in me that beareth not fruit he taketh away: and every branch that beareth fruit, he purgeth it, that it may bring forth more fruit" (John 15:2). This principle is also corroborated by the writer to the Hebrews, "Now no chastening for the present seemeth to be joyous, but grievous: nevertheless afterward it yieldeth the peaceable fruit of righteousness unto them which are exercised thereby" (Hebrews 12:11). A life that has known and felt the chastening hand of God is a life that produces fruit.

Recounting his experiences in the belly of the fish, Jonah was honest enough to admit that none other than the hand of God had been upon his life, even though it was during the time of his disobedience. According to Paul, God's ultimate purpose is to conform us to the exact image Jesus Christ (Romans 8:29,30). In the process of conforming us to the image of the Lord Jesus, God is able to make all the events of our lives to work together toward this purpose. When we know that God is at work in us for this purpose then we can begin to understand the benefit we derive from affliction and persecution. Was it for this reason Paul wrote, "We glory in tribulations also: knowing that tribulation worketh patience; And patience, experience; and experience, hope: And hope maketh not ashamed; because the love of God is shed abroad in our hearts by the Holy Ghost which is given unto us" (Romans 5:3-5)?

In her book, *"A Step Further"*, Joni Erickson Tada says, "I really don't mind the inconvenience of being paralysed if my faithfulness to God, while in this wheelchair, will bring glory to Him." Joni continues, "But today as I look back, I am convinced that the whole ordeal of my paralysis was inspired by His love. I wasn't a rat in a maze. I wasn't the brunt of some cruel divine joke. God had reasons behind my suffering, learning some of them has made all the difference in the world."

Ten years ago I spoke at the funeral service of a dear colleague in the gospel. I remember how through the days of this brother's affliction and fight with leukaemia he bore a great witness to the gospel and through that witness many believers were restored and sinners converted.

Undoubtedly, Jonah strode out from God's presence in defiance and disobedience, but the Lord had a chastening hand on the prophet. This prophecy is like a beacon by which God teaches us, and Jonah testifies of the lessons he learned in the school of disobedience.

Jonah learned to have a new sense of compassion. There is a noticeable contrast between chapter one and chapter two. In the first chapter Jonah was rudely awakened by the captain and must have thought to himself, *Who does this Gentile dog think he is and why are these pagans calling upon their gods? Salvation comes from Israel and ends with Israel.*

Repentance is a change of mind and most certainly Jonah had a different attitude in chapter two. He began to recognise how compassionate God had been to him and then manifested compassion on the heathen Gentiles as he cried, "Those that cling to worthless idols forfeit the grace that could be theirs" (Jonah 2:8). This is the first suggestion of any compassion the prophet displayed for the pagan Ninevites, a concern which should have burned with passion in his soul from the beginning of the story. Like his Lord and Saviour, Jonah begins to see the Ninevites as "*sheep without a Shepherd.*"

Like Jonah and the Saviour, we also are confronted with the needs of fallen humanity day after day. Do we display the love of Christ? Consider Paul's burden and passion for his fellow countrymen, "I say the truth in Christ, I lie not, my conscience also bearing me witness in the Holy Ghost, That I have great heaviness and continual sorrow in my heart. For I could wish that myself were accursed from Christ for my brethren, my kinsmen according to the flesh...Brethren, my heart's desire and prayer to God for Israel is, that they might be saved" (Romans 9:1-3, 10:1).

A minister of the gospel, Theodore Cuyler, wanted to learn all he could about Robert M. McCheyne. So he asked an elderly gentleman who knew him, "Can you tell me about some of the messages, some of the texts that McCheyne used?"

The man replied, "I'm sorry, I don't remember."

"Don't you recall anything about him?" asked Cuyler.

"Oh, that's a different question," said the old believer, "I will never forget the time Robert McCheyne came to visit our home when I was just a lad. Mr McCheyne said, 'James, I have come to visit your sick sister.' Then he looked into my eyes and added with deep emotion, 'And James, I am very concerned about your soul.' Sir, I have forgotten his messages but I can still feel the tremble of his hand and see the tears in his eyes. His compassion for my soul resulted in my conversion."

Jonah learned a new sense of consecration. After his repentance Jonah wanted to revisit and fulfil his promises; "I will pay that that I have vowed" (Jonah 2:9). Jonah looked back to a previous day in his life, perhaps the day God called him to be a prophet, when he vowed a vow unto God. Possibly he said something like, "Lord, I'll go wherever you want me to go, say whatever you want me to say, do whatever you want me to do." Whatever the vow, Jonah had violated that pledge when he forsook God's way and fled for Tarshish. Now, deep in the belly of the fish he renewed his promise to fulfil that vow.

Jonah was not the sort of prodigal who prayed, "Lord, if I ever get out of here I will live differently, I will pay that which I have vowed." God holds us accountable to the promises we make to Him when we are in a tight corner. At such times it is better not to vow than to vow and not keep it.

Jonah learned to *sing God's praise*. We are not told if Jonah was a baritone or tenor. Whatever his voice, he now wanted to sing and make melody in his heart unto the Lord. I think he must have sung the Psalms for he already quoted them so freely. He offered, "I will sacrifice unto thee with the voice of thanksgiving" (Jonah 2:9).

The scriptures remind us that "Whoso offereth praise glorifieth God (Psalm 50:23). Paul commanded, "In everything give thanks for this is will of God in Christ Jesus concerning you" (1 Thessalonians 5:8). Most of our thanksgiving is associated with good times, times with the family or bringing in the harvest. Jonah must have learned the liberating habit of giving thanks in everything. Job also greatly illustrates how praise helps us through our calamities. Job lost his family, his farm and his fortune, yet he gave thanks and prayed, "The Lord gave, and the Lord hath taken away, blessed be the name of the Lord" (Job 1:21).

Paul and Silas had been beaten publicly in Philippi after which they were cast into a dark, damp and dirty dungeon of a prison. They had ample reason to complain or murmur. Instead, "At midnight Paul and Silas prayed and sang praises unto God" (Acts 16:25). Praise and thanksgiving were the very keys that unlocked those prison doors which resulted in the jailor and his family trusting Christ as Saviour.

Learn to praise the Lord and sing songs in the night seasons of our lives. They will help us through until that day breaks and the shadows forever flee away.

A DELIVERED LIFE PROMISES HOPE

When the Lord delivered Jonah from the dark depths of a watery grave, the prophet acknowledged the great and sovereign hand of God. The prophet shouted, "'Salvation is of the Lord.' And the Lord spake unto the fish, and it vomited out Jonah upon the dry land" (Jonah 2:9-10).

Things would never be the same again for Jonah. After the penitent Jonah prayed in the belly of the fish, the prodigal prophet became the pardoned prophet. When this forgiven fugitive cried, "Salvation is of the Lord", he acknowledged several things:

In relation to himself, Jonah was helpless. Down in the belly of the fish the prophet was totally helpless. While he was on dry land, and even in the hold of the ship, Jonah might have been able to pull a few strings here and there to gain some respectability for his actions. Maybe he even could have attributed his survival to his own efforts. However, when he was down in the belly of the fish he was as good as dead, there was nothing he could do. He needed a resurrection, the miracle of God's salvation.

That is exactly how it is with our salvation. The human condition is so weak that we are counted as those who are spiritually dead. Nothing short of a miracle, a resurrection, could save us. That is exactly what God has done for us, "Even when we were dead in sins, hath quickened us together with Christ, (by grace ye are saved;) and hath raised us up together, and made us sit together in heavenly places in Christ Jesus" (Ephesians 2:5-6).

In relation to God, Jonah was hopeful. It was only when Jonah was brought to the depths of despair that he began to see the Lord again. It is for that reason he cried, "I am cast out of thy sight; yet I will look again toward thy holy temple" (Jonah 2:4). Spurgeon made this comment about afflictions that cast us totally on the Lord,

> "In seasons of severe trial, the Christian has nothing on earth that he can trust, and is therefore compelled to cast himself on his God alone. When his vessel is on its beam-ends, and no human deliverance can avail, he must simply and entirely trust himself to the providence and care of God. Happy storm that wrecks a man on such a rock as this! O blessed hurricane that drives the soul to God and God alone! There is no getting at our God sometimes because of the multitude of our friends; but when a man is so poor, so friendless, so helpless that he has nowhere else to turn, he flies

into his Father's arms, and is blessedly clasped therein! When he is burdened with troubles so pressing and so peculiar, that he cannot tell them to any but his God, he may be thankful for them; for he will learn more of his Lord then than at any other time. Oh, tempest-tossed believer, it is a happy trouble that drives thee to thy Father!"

It is interesting that Jonah mentioned the temple in his prayer. He proceeded to entreat God by remembering the appeal that was made to God at the dedication of the temple in Jerusalem, "What prayer and supplication soever be made by any man, or by all thy people Israel, which shall know every man the plague of his own heart, and spread forth his hands toward this house: Then hear thou in heaven thy dwelling place, and forgive, and do, and give to every man according to his ways" (1 Kings 8:38, 39).

Jonah further expressed his hope and expectation for deliverance by God when he mourned, "When my soul fainted within me I remembered the Lord: and my prayer came in unto thee, into thine holy temple" (Jonah 2:7).

One of the most moving events in the history of the Christian church took place in the middle of the 16th century in Scotland. The church was being persecuted and Mary Queen of Scots was doing everything she could to stamp out the revival which was causing the Reformation to sweep through Scotland. It seemed there was no man available to challenge or stop her sanguineous rampage. The only man who might have been able to stand up to the monarch was in Geneva learning reformation theology at the feet of John Calvin. One day Calvin called young John Knox and said to him, "It is time for you to go to Scotland."

In the meantime the people in Scotland were praying that God would somehow deliver them from the Queen's scourge. John Knox arrived in Scotland in answer to their prayers. Soon word spread across the lowlands and highlands, "John Knox has come, Knox has come." The population was electrified as Scotland became inflamed with joy and hope at the arrival of this man of God. John Knox stood for God against Romish heresy and against Mary's conspiracy by which the Monarch tried to impose false religion on the land. Soon Mary Queen of Scots was heard to say that she feared the prayers of John Knox more than an army of 10,000 men.

God rescued Scotland when the people cried, pleaded and prayed unto God. He heard their cry and sent deliverance to the land.

God is able to deliver individuals who cry unto Him as He is also able to deliver nations that turn to Him, "Salvation is of the Lord" (Jonah 2:9).

9 FAILURE IS NOT FINAL
Jonah 3:1-4

"The victorious Christian life," said George H. Morrison, "is a series of new beginnings." Satan would have us believe that when we fail it is the end of our ministry without any hope of recovery. However, the testimony that comes from Jonah and many other Bible characters is that our God is the God of the second chance.

Isaiah prophesied that despite Judah's coming captivity by the Babylonians, God would not forsake His people, "Remember ye not the former things, neither consider the things of old. Behold, I will do a new thing; now it shall spring forth; shall ye not know it? I will even make a way in the wilderness, and rivers in the desert" (Isaiah 43:18-19).

In like manner, although Jonah was literally "all washed up", yet it was not the end of the prophet or his ministry for, "The word of the Lord came unto Jonah the second time" (Jonah 3:1). I find it amazing that the Lord should speak to Jonah at all. After all, Jonah had turned his back on God, on His will and had disobeyed His Word. The Lord had to take drastic measures involving thunder, rain, a stormy sea, frightened mariners and a large fish to bring the man of God to his senses and subsequently, to repentance. It was after Jonah confessed his sins and returned to the Lord that he was able to hear the voice of God again.

We may not know on what shore the great fish deposited Jonah, but we can imagine that after his rude expulsion from the convulsing fish, the prophet picked himself up on some unfamiliar seashore, wiped the seaweed from his face and wondered where he was. I wonder did he begin to ponder some other questions that might have troubled his mind, *"Will God use me again? Will God call me again? Will God bless me again?"* The answer to these questions came with a resounding affirmative, "The Word of the Lord came unto Jonah the second time."

Jonah was not alone in receiving the mercy of a second chance. Reading through the scriptures we find many great champions who needed God's forgiveness, mercy and restoration to their ministry. Abraham fled to Egypt, where he lied about his wife, yet God gave him another chance and brought him back to Canaan. Jacob deceived his father Isaac about his identity, yet God forgave him and used him to build the nation of Israel. After Moses killed an Egyptian he fled from Egypt, but God followed him and called him to be the greatest leader of His people at a most important time in history. Three times Peter denied his Lord with oaths and curses, but the Risen Lord Jesus singled him out, forgave him and said, "Feed my sheep." Young John Mark forsook Paul and Barnabas on their first missionary journey, but God still used him to write the Gospel record that bears his name and even Paul spoke highly of him just prior to the apostle's own execution.

The best of God's servants have made foolish mistakes, but God did not forsake them, nor will He forsake you. How many times have you felt you are a washout, a flop and total failure? In spite of our failures it is good to know that God does not discard of us nor is He through with us yet. Personally, I am glad that our God is the God of the second chance for I have needed to know that many times in my ministry.

There are three things I want to note about Jonah's second chance.

GOD GAVE A MANDATE THAT IS SUGGESTIVE

God commanded Jonah, "Arise, go unto Nineveh, that great city, and preach unto it the preaching that I bid thee" (Jonah 3:2). This command suggests several things to me:

God treats his workers graciously. God is always more concerned about His workers than about their work. If the worker is what he ought to be, then the work will be what it ought to be. Throughout Jonah's time of rebellion, God was displeased with His servant, but God did not hold spite against the prophet. The Lord harbours no resentment or hard feelings when we digress from the way He indicates for us.

Jonah knew that God was gracious and later described His character, "I knew that thou art a gracious God, and merciful, slow to anger, and of great kindness, and repentest thee of the evil" (Jonah 4:2). It was because of His grace that God came to Jonah the second time, recommissioning, restoring and reinstating Jonah to prophetic service.

Some years ago God greatly used a very capable evangelist in the British Isles. Sadly, he went into spiritual decline, lost his interest in spiritual matters and drifted into sin for a number of months. The sin in which he indulged at first was committed in secret, but soon it became public knowledge and even made the headlines in the newspapers. At first, all he could think of was how he had been ruined for life. After some prolonged anguish he finally realised what a fool he had been to sin against the Lord and, like the prodigal, he returned to the Lord from the pigpen of disaster. When he returned to the Lord the evangelist discovered exactly what the prodigal had found many years earlier and what Jonah also encountered in his day; the Lord not only welcomed him back, but began to strengthen and bless him.

After a period of waiting, the preacher felt constrained to return to public ministry, but was afraid that his debacle and decline would become a public scandal. Convinced that his hidden secret had not been found out, he went back to preaching, rejoicing in the forgiveness of God.

One night when he was in Aberdeen, he was given a sealed letter just before the service began. He began to read the unsigned letter, which described a shameful series of events in which he had been engaged earlier in life. His stomach churned as he read, "If you have the gall to preach tonight, I will stand and expose you."

The evangelist took the letter and went to his knees. A few minutes later he was in the pulpit with the letter still in his hand. To the assembled congregation he read the shameful letter in full. Then he said, "I want to make it perfectly clear that this letter is true. I am ashamed of what I have done. I come tonight not as one who is perfect, but as one who is forgiven."

God greatly used the rest of that evangelist's ministry. His enthusiastic preaching became like a mighty magnet, drawing people to Christ. God is gracious in His dealing with His children. The Psalmist said it well, "Like as a father pitieth his children, so the Lord pitieth them that fear him. For he knoweth our frame; he remembereth that we are dust" (Psalm 103:13-14).

God takes His witness seriously. God's second command to Jonah was similar to that which came to him the first time. At the beginning God had said, "Arise, go to Nineveh" (Jonah 1:2). After Jonah's deliverance from the fish, God said, "Arise, go unto Nineveh, that great city, and preach unto it the preaching that I bid thee" (Jonah 3:2). Jonah may have thought that his excursion to the Mediterranean would cause God to forget about His original command to go to Nineveh, or even change His mind about the mission. Jonah soon discovered that when God said, "Go," He meant it. Paul later said to the Romans, "The gifts and calling of God are without repentance" (Romans 11:29).

Just as God's Word to Jonah had not changed, so also the great "Go" of the Saviour's Great Commission has not been rescinded. Jesus Christ said, "Go ye into all the world and preach the gospel to every creature" (Mark 16:15). Someone has said, "To know the gospel is to owe the gospel. To owe the gospel is to go with the gospel."

The president of a large bank heard an evangelist talking about soul-winning. Afterwards he said to the evangelist, "I have a cashier who is not a Christian. Will you come and speak to him about salvation?"

The evangelist answered, "If I speak to him he will just take it from me as my professional task, but if you speak to him about the Saviour, he will know that you have a personal interest in Him."

"All right," said the banker, "I will speak to him, but you come with me."

The next morning the evangelist went to the banker's office and the cashier was called in. The president introduced him to the evangelist and then said, "I want to talk to you about the most important thing in the world, your relationship to Jesus Christ." The cashier wanted to know if it was more important than deposits and loans and all the business of the bank. "Yes it is," said the president.

The cashier replied, "Then why haven't you told me about it before now?"

Do we take the Great Commission seriously? Jonah took God seriously the second time He spoke.

Jonah trusted God's Word primarily. The primary instrument God uses in the salvation of sinners is His Word, the written and spoken. Some might wish that there was some other way that God would save men. Salvation does not come by human wisdom, secular reason, dramatic signs or slick entertainment. God has decreed that men are to be saved by preaching. Paul wrote, "For after that in the wisdom of God the world by wisdom knew not God, it pleased God by the foolishness of preaching to save them that believe" (1 Corinthians 1:21). Again Paul emphasized, "Woe is me if I preach not the gospel" (1 Corinthians 9:16).

Jonah was a well-respected prophet but his preaching was governed by the word God gave to him. That is why we read as follows, "Arise, go unto Nineveh, that great city, and preach unto it the preaching that I bid thee" (Jonah 3:2). The only kind of preaching that God owns and blesses is that which He commands. We are not given a choice of what to preach and the pulpit is not a place to propagate a preacher's peculiar views on social, political or economical affairs. The true servant of Christ must follow the pattern God has ordained, "preach the Word" (2 Timothy 4:2).

Fellow preachers, in an age when the Word of God is being relegated, substituted or replaced, we need to affirm our commitment to the authority and centrality of the Bible. Perhaps you say, "I like to hear good preaching." Preaching and witnessing is something that we often leave to others, but it is also something we can do.

Furthermore, God did not send Jonah to engage in 'lifestyle evangelism' in Nineveh. He simply said, "Arise, go unto Nineveh that great city and preach" (Jonah 3:2). Preaching does not necessarily mean that you have to be an articulate orator, but it does mean that there must be a willingness to share Christ wherever you go.

GOD FOUND A MESSENGER WHO IS RESPONSIVE

When God called Jonah the second time, the repentant prophet gave a willing and immediate response, "So Jonah arose, and went unto Nineveh, according to the word of the Lord. Now Nineveh was an exceeding great city of three days' journey" (Jonah 3:3). This was in stark contrast to how the prophet had responded before. When God previously said, "Arise, go to Nineveh", Jonah fled in the opposite direction. With repentance there had been a complete change of mind and the prophet was now on his way to Nineveh. Earlier Jonah, "rose... to flee from the presence of the Lord," but now Jonah "arose... and went according to the Word of the Lord."

Jonah was moved by the truth. Jonah's human and prejudiced reasoning had made him flee from God's command, but after the ordeal inside the fish, the Word of God came unto him the second time and charged him with the same great mission he had tried to avoid. When God said, "Go," to Jonah the first time, He meant it. When God came to him the second time it was with the same charge, "Go unto Nineveh."

I am convinced that Jonah's journey to Nineveh was the happiest he had ever made in his life. The trip on the Mediterranean held no happiness for Jonah; on the contrary, it was fraught with tragedy. The prophet only found peace and contentment by going to Nineveh in the will of God.

Fear made Jonah flee "from the presence of the Lord," and in doing so he followed the dictates of his own heart. Now, the man of God arises to go to Nineveh, "according to the Word of the Lord." Nothing else moved Jonah apart from the Word of God. Nothing other than glad surrender and submission to the will of God can satisfy the soul or heal its wounds.

Jonah was made for the times. Someone has said, "Most people are made *by* the times, few are made *for* the times, but all God's people are made *for* the times." The problem is that the Church of Jesus Christ has been swallowed up by the spirit of this age. We have allowed "the world around us to squeeze us into its mould" (Romans 12:2). The Lord Jesus said, "Ye are the salt of the earth...Ye are the light of the world" (Matthew 5:13-14), but we have failed in these roles. We are not seasoning society nor are we are giving a clear light to the world. Instead of being "made for the times, we are being made by the times."

Jonah was a man made for his time. God selected him to do a great work in Nineveh.

Four times in this book Nineveh is called "a great city" (Jonah 1:2; 3:2-3; 4:11). Nineveh was great in size for it was "*a city of three days journey*" (Jonah 3:3). The population of Nineveh numbered into hundreds of thousands and the city covered an area of some sixty square miles. Reference to "three days journey" might infer that it took a three day visit to see greater Nineveh. The city was great in splendour, the greatest city of the powerful Assyrian Empire.

Nineveh was also a city of great sin. This is referred to at the beginning of the prophecy, "Arise, go to Nineveh, that great city, and cry against it; for their wickedness is come up before me" (Jonah 1:2). Archaeologists have discovered that Nineveh was one of the most sinful of history. The Assyrians were brutal, impaling their victims while still alive on sharp poles and leaving them to roast to death in the desert sun. They beheaded people by the thousands and stacked their skulls up in piles by the city gates. These Assyrians even skinned people alive. They were an exceedingly violent, vicious and vice-filled people.

It was to this "great city" that God sent one man for a city-wide evangelistic crusade with a message of judgement. This was not like present day evangelistic campaigns where posters advertise the event and invite the populace to an arena or large building. There was no well-oiled planning committee or sponsorship for the prophet. He cut a lonely figure standing alone on the streets of this large city preaching to the passers-by.

Jonah did a job that no one else could do. That is why God sent Jonah and no one else.

God also has something for you to do that no one else can do. He not only gives us a work to do, but will also give the grace to do it; "But unto every one of us is given grace according to the measure of the gift of Christ" (Ephesians 4:7). Do not be fearful that the Lord will ask you to go somewhere that you cannot face. The saying is true, "The will of God will never lead you where the grace of God can't keep you and the power of God can't use you."

A MINISTRY WHICH IS EFFECTIVE

Subsequent to Jonah obeying God and going to Nineveh, an amazing thing happened, "The people of Nineveh believed God" (Jonah 3:5). Not only did God shake Jonah back to his senses, He also stirred the Ninevites and brought about a mighty awakening in the city. From the palace to the pauper, it seemed there was universal and genuine repentance throughout Nineveh, "So the people of Nineveh believed God, and proclaimed a fast, and put on sackcloth, from the greatest of them even to the least of them. For word came unto the king of Nineveh, and he arose from his throne, and he laid his robe from him, and covered him with sackcloth, and sat in ashes. And he caused it to be proclaimed and published through Nineveh by the decree of the king and his nobles, saying,

Let neither man nor beast, herd nor flock, taste any thing: let them not feed, nor drink water: But let man and beast be covered with sackcloth, and cry mightily unto God: yea, let them turn every one from his evil way, and from the violence that is in their hands" (Jonah 3:5-8).

Think of what would happen if God would send such an awakening to our nation today. We certainly need it. I feel that nothing short of a great spiritual revival will provide any hope for multitudes of people outside our churches. Perhaps it is even more important to observe that without a great awakening of God's people inside our churches, there is little hope for a stirring in the hearts of the unconverted outside. We need revival.

Why did Jonah's ministry so shake Nineveh? I think there are several reasons:

There was urgency to Jonah's mission and ministry. Although the city was of "three days journey", Jonah began to preach as soon as he found opportunity in the city, "Jonah began to enter into the city a day's journey, and he cried, and said, Yet forty days, and Nineveh shall be overthrown" (Jonah 3:4).

Can you picture this preacher calling to the very first person or group of people he met and beginning to proclaim the message of judgement to them, "Yet forty days, and Nineveh shall be overthrown" (Jonah 3:4).

While on holiday a few years ago I met an unforgettable character from the city of York, England. His name was Tommy Goat and he used to walk through the city preaching the gospel. The authorities got quite annoyed with his unusual activity and actually imprisoned him on a charge of public disorder. They thought he was crazy but Tommy was just doing what Jonah did many centuries earlier.

Jonah wasted no time in obeying God or warning the people of impending judgement. We also should be mindful that God "hath appointed a day, in the which he will judge the world in righteousness by that man whom he hath ordained; whereof he hath given assurance unto all men, in that he hath raised him from the dead" (Acts 17:31). Human necessity and a sense of urgency should motivate us to engage in warning "every man, and teaching every man in all wisdom; that we may present every man perfect in Christ Jesus" (Colossians 1:28).

The Lord Jesus said, "Say not ye, there are yet four months and then cometh harvest? Behold I say unto you lift up your eyes and look on the fields for they are white already to harvest" (John 4:35).

There was a transparency in Jonah's his ministry. In the belly of the fish Jonah had learned to passionately cry out to God. With equal fervency Jonah cried out to the people of Nineveh to flee from the wrath to come. The voice that Jonah raised in urgent and desperate prayer when he was alone in the fish's belly was now employed to preach with similar urgency and fervour in the public place. Someone has said, "We can tell what we are by what we do when we are alone." When Jonah was alone, "he cried unto God". What he was in the secret place was balanced by what he did on the streets of Nineveh. His ministry was transparent and free from any pretence.

Paul reminds us that, "Whatsoever ye do, do it heartily, as to the Lord, and not unto men" (Colossians 3:23). Whatever you do for Him, make sure you follow what Paul prayed for the Philippian Christians, "That ye may approve things that are excellent; that ye may be sincere and without offence till the day of Christ" (Philippians 1:10).

10

WHAT CAN ONE PERSON DO?
Jonah 3:1-10

The Bible gives us abundant evidence of what one solitary person can do to change his or her world. Consider Moses who, after hearing God speak from a burning bush, went back to Egypt and became the emancipator of God's enslaved people. Think about Nehemiah who, after hearing the report from his brethren of broken down walls and burnt out gates in Jerusalem, left his high and privileged position in the palace to go back to Jerusalem and lead the people in rebuilding the city.

William Wilberforce, one of Great Britain's greatest Prime Ministers virtually single-handedly brought an end to slavery and the slave trade in this nation over a century ago. The influence of one man can also be measured when we consider the life of Jonah. In spite of the fact that he had failed and disobeyed God, there is no doubt that this one man's ministry dramatically changed the course of history for Nineveh and transformed the lives and homes of the Ninevites.

Perhaps back in Gath-hepher, the prophet's home town, the people must have wagged their heads as they lamented, "Jonah is finished. God will never use him again." God did use him again to bring about one of the greatest revivals in history, but it all began when this one man repented and got right with God.

The same principle is not only important, it still is imperative for revival today. When God's people repent from their disobedience and return to Him, God has promised to bless them and their land, "If my people, which are called by my name, shall humble themselves, and pray, and seek my face, and turn from their wicked ways; then will I hear from heaven, and will forgive their sin, and will heal their land" (2 Chronicles 7:14).

You could be the key to a spiritual awakening in your church or your community. The famous American evangelist, D. L. Moody, was first a shoe salesman and a Sunday school teacher before he became an evangelist. The first time he came to England he made very little impression on the population. However, during that visit he heard a young man, a Mr Varley, preach in a field. During his discourse the open-air English preacher said, "The world is yet to see what God can do with one man who is wholly and totally committed to Him."

Moody replied, "I will be that man." And he was! He yielded his all to God and the mighty anointing of God came upon him and transformed his ministry.

Two very graphic pictures are brought before us in this passage:

JONAH WAS A PEDESTRIAN PREACHER

From a human perspective, Jonah's mission to Nineveh might have appeared ridiculous. How could one man, claiming to be the prophet of an unknown Deity, confront hundreds of thousands of people with his strange and unattractive message of judgement, and ever be accepted in this foreign capital? How could a Jew, who worshipped the only true God, ever constrain these barbaric and idolatrous Gentiles to believe what he preached? For all he knew, Jonah could fall into the hands of these barbarians, be impaled on a stake or skinned alive like countless others.

Notwithstanding the difficulties and absurdity, Jonah went to Nineveh in obedience to his Lord. Perhaps fearlessly, most certainly faithfully, he preached on the public thoroughfares, "And Jonah began to enter into the city a day's journey, and he cried, and said,

"Yet forty days, and Nineveh shall be overthrown" (Jonah 3:4). Jonah's message literally meant that Nineveh would be turned upside down, the city would be totally destroyed, as were Sodom and Gomorrah.

We are not sure if this was all that Jonah said in his sermon, but we note that his message was short, simple, searching and startling. Perhaps the prophet also took time to tell the people about the true and living God for we read, "The people of Nineveh believed God" (Jonah 3:5). True faith is not exercised in the dark. The people needed to have some understanding about the God of Israel in order to believe in Him. Jonah must have also exposed the folly of idolatry for they forsook their idols. Maybe he also recounted to them his own personal history to emphasise just how powerful and sovereign the Lord is.

We simply don't know how much Jonah might have expanded his message. All we know is that he obeyed God, went to Nineveh, declared the message God had given him. It was God who touched their hearts and granted repentance to the Ninevites.

Here was a prophet who preached the Word of God faithfully. When God said to Jonah, "Preach unto Nineveh", we find that he cried "yet forty days and Nineveh shall be overthrown" (Jonah 3:4). Much and all as the prophet might only have wanted to make a one-day visit to Nineveh, yet he remained in the great city for an extended period, even though he was pronouncing judgement on its people.

Throughout Scripture, the number forty seems to be identified with testing or judgement. During the time of Noah, it rained forty days and forty nights (Genesis 7:4 12, 17). When Moses sent the spies to explore Canaan they were there for forty days (Numbers 14:34). Moses led the children of Israel through forty years of testing in the wilderness (Deuteronomy 2:7). The defiant giant Goliath taunted the army of Israel for forty days before he was slain by David (1 Samuel 17:16). The Saviour was driven by the Spirit into the wilderness for forty days and forty nights, "Then was Jesus led up of the Spirit into the wilderness to be tempted of the devil" (Matthew

4:1). It is therefore significant that the Lord gave forty days to the people of Nineveh to repent and turn from their wickedness.

Jonah had to be faithful to stay in Nineveh and keep on preaching the Word of God even though the task seemed formidable. His message was not some compromising, watered-down, mamby-pamby, candy-coated sermonette. No. Here was a man who sensed his obligation to be faithful to the Word of God and warn the people.

Jonah is an example for all preachers. We live in an age when society and some people in the pew want to dictate to the preacher. Social pressures press in on the man of God in the pulpit, attempting to mould his thinking and attitudes. The true servant of Christ must always, "Preach the word; be instant in season, out of season" (2 Timothy 4:2). The preacher's attitude should be that of Paul, "If I pleased men I should not be the servant of Christ" (Galatians 1:10).

Jonah's brief was for forty days and the message was about coming judgement from God. Even though the message was not popular the prophet knew he had to be faithful to God who sent him.

One of Satan's foremost lies today is that the message of judgement frightens people away from church. In our post modern and plastic society men and women still want to know the truth. Some churches have adopted a "seeker-friendly" strategy whereby they avoid speaking of such things as judgement and wrath to come. They feel that the so called "hell fire preaching" of a hundred years ago is not for this present time. The result is that many churches are empty, Christians have lost their fervour and the Word of God has been neglected.

On one of the small islands in the Shetlands there are spectacular cliffs where the birds flock in their hundreds. Often tourists go to watch them. Sometimes, however, a major tragedy occurs. While walking along the cliffs some visitors fail to notice where the slippery grass suddenly stops and the cliffs begin. Without warning, the unsuspecting visitor can take one step on solid ground, but then the next tragic footfall could be over the cliff face with disastrous results.

If a local resident saw a visitor approaching the edge of the cliff do you think it would be melodramatic for him to shout a warning? Of course not. It would be the right thing to do. That is exactly how

Jonah felt. He already knew it was "a fearful thing to fall into the hands of the living God" (Hebrews 10:31). The prophet preached to warn the Ninevites of impending judgement. Jesus Christ said that Jonah's experience in the belly of the fish was like a warning beacon to the people of Nineveh, "For as Jonas was a sign unto the Ninevites, so shall also the Son of man be to this generation" (Luke 11:30).

Here was a prophet who preached the Word of God clearly. There was simplicity and clarity in Jonah's preaching, "Yet forty days, and Nineveh shall be overthrown" (Jonah 3:4). You would not have needed an advanced degree in Mesopotamian culture and languages from Nineveh's university to understand what this prophet from Galilee was saying. His message was clear, plain, lucid and unambiguous.

Someone has said, "If you ever want a lesson in ambiguity, listen to a liberal preacher." Sadly, many who occupy the pulpits of our land have no experience of God's saving grace or an intimate acquaintance with Jesus Christ. Without the benefit of speaking from personal experience or conviction, their message is often a masterpiece of obscurity. Too many evangelical preachers preach the gospel with their eye on the saints. They preach to please and impress the converted.

The God-given task of any evangelist is to present and preach God's Word to their contemporaries so that it can be clearly comprehended. I believe we should preach so that if our hearer has never heard the gospel before, he will clearly understand; if he never hears the gospel again, he will never forget it. Every occasion for preaching is vital. Paul spoke of not, "handling the word of God deceitfully; but by manifestation of the truth commending ourselves to every man's conscience in the sight of God" (2 Corinthians 4:2). That is exactly what Jonah did.

Here was a prophet who preached the Word of God persuasively. I wonder did it surprise Jonah, when after he preached, "the people of Nineveh believed God" (Jonah 3:5)? The Ninevites listened to the prophet and looked at Jonah. Could it be that the effects of his three-day stay in the belly of the fish had made him such a horrifying sight to behold? Perhaps the appearance of this foreign prophet made them exclaim, "God punishes sin. Look at this prophet, he is discoloured. God must have punished him." Likewise, the fact that Jonah was alive at all might have caused them to add, "God also pardons sinners for God spared this disobedient prophet."

Jonah was preaching after his own personal experience of the reality of God's judgement. It was for that reason that the prophet preached with an expectancy for God to work. Too frequently we preach without an anticipation of God working. We fail to expect anything unusual or beyond the norm. A young student came to C. H. Spurgeon on one occasion and said, "Mr Spurgeon I have been preaching around the countryside now for some time, but I don't see souls saved like you do."

Spurgeon looked at the young man and asked, "Do you expect to see souls saved every time you preach?"

The young preacher replied, "Why, no sir."

To this Spurgeon said, "That is why you don't see people saved."

Perhaps Jonah was not surprised when the Ninevites believed. According to chapter 4:2 he expected them to believe and benefit from the mercy of God, "And he prayed unto the Lord, and said, I pray thee, O Lord, was not this my saying, when I was yet in my country? Therefore I fled before unto Tarshish: for I knew that thou art a gracious God, and merciful, slow to anger, and of great kindness, and repentest thee of the evil" (Jonah 4:2). When we are as persuaded of God's truth as we ought to be, there will be a contagious persuasion that will prevail on others. I must therefore ask if you are persuaded of what you believe? Are you unshakeable in the truths that have been revealed to us in the scriptures?

THE NINEVITES BECAME A PENITENT PEOPLE

What would we say if a lone preacher from the West were to preach the gospel in Beijing and witness a mass revival, which issued in the conversion of the Chinese authorities and a directive from the ruling hierarchy that abolished state atheism in favour of complete freedom for the worship of God and the preaching of Christ? Do you believe such things could happen?

That is a precise parallel to the impact of what happened in the ancient world when the people of Nineveh turned from their idolatry and heathenism to seek the living God. Jonah recorded the magnitude of the great revival, "So the people of Nineveh believed God, and proclaimed a fast, and put on sackcloth, from the greatest of them even to the least of them" (Jonah 3:5).

God had a plan for Nineveh and Jonah was not able to frustrate it even though he rebelled at first. That was the very reason why God chastened Jonah. Chastening was not given for its own sake. It never is. God had a plan for Nineveh and Jonah's adjustment was part of that plan.

The Lord still deals with us in that same way. He brings us through *"fiery trials"*, not only to make us more Christ-like, but ultimately that we might be channels of blessing to others, "He comforteth us in all our tribulation, that we may be able to comfort them which are in any trouble, by the comfort wherewith we ourselves are comforted of God" (2 Corinthians 1:4). We can therefore understand why Jonah was a comfort and help to the Ninevites. Jesus later indicated the influence of the preacher, "They repented at the preaching of Jonah" (Luke 11:32).

Repentance in Nineveh was total. Repentance (*metanoeo* Gk) means "to change one's mind." To repent is a turning from sin which involves an intellectual exercise that changes the mind, an emotional experience with a change of heart, and a volitional experience with a change of will. God in heaven witnessed and testified to the validity of their repentance by adjourning judgement, "And God saw their works, that they turned from their evil way; and God repented of the evil, that he had said that he would do unto them; and he did it not" (Jonah 3:10).

Genuine repentance not only brings a change of mind but also produces genuine sorrow for sin and an aversion to the sin of which the penitent repented. Paul indicated this when he wrote to the Corinthians, "Now I rejoice, not that ye were made sorry, but that ye sorrowed to repentance: for ye were made sorry after a godly manner" (2 Corinthians 7:9). Genuine repentance always brings a response of mercy and forgiveness with the Lord.

Note the following features of repentance in Nineveh:

Repentance by the Ninevites was prompt. With the Ninevites there was no delay in turning to God. As soon as Jonah cried, "Yet forty days, and Nineveh shall be overthrown" Jonah (3:4), the people of Nineveh immediately "believed God" and repented. Promptness is the only way to react to God's message because postponing repentance invites divine judgement.

This immediate response to the prophet's proclamation reminds us of Paul's word to the Corinthians, "Behold *now* is the accepted time; behold, *now* is the day of salvation" (2 Corinthians 6:2). When God calls to repentance, it is time to repent.

Repentance by the Ninevites was public. I find it amazing that when one man got right with God a whole city repented. When one man corrected his ways, he changed his world. After Jonah came to the Lord in penitence the whole city of Nineveh came to the Lord in repentance. From the King on his throne to the very beasts in the field Nineveh was filled with penitence and change, "So the people of Nineveh believed God, and proclaimed a fast, and put on sackcloth, from the greatest of them even to the least of them. For word came unto the king of Nineveh, and he arose from his throne, and he laid his robe from him, and covered him with sackcloth, and sat in ashes. And he caused it to be proclaimed and published through Nineveh by the decree of the king and his nobles, saying, Let neither man nor beast, herd nor flock, taste any thing: let them not feed, nor drink water" (Jonah 3:6-7).

Think of what could happen in our nation if God's people were to repent of their secret sin. It is when God's people turn to God in repentance that God follows with revival. There is no other way. Repentance in the church could touch the monarch in the palace or the prime minister in his office.

A one-sentence sermon from the penitent prophet and Nineveh was brought to its knees. Did you know that the same thing happened in our land during the days of the 1859 Revival in Ulster? The well-known Ulster evangelist and author, J. Edwin Orr, told of a schoolboy in Coleraine who was under deep conviction of sin. Incapable of continuing his studies, his teacher sent him home in the company of another boy who was already a Christian. On their way home the two boys noticed an empty house and they entered it to pray.

After some time, the unsaved boy trusted Christ as Saviour and immediately returned to the classroom to tell his teacher, "I am so happy I have the Lord Jesus in my heart."

That simple testimony had a dynamic effect on the whole class and boy after boy stepped outside to get right with God. The confused teacher looked out of the window and observed the boys kneeling in prayer around the school yard. Finally, the teacher also was overcome and asked the converted schoolboy to speak to the entire class.

Soon the whole school was in disarray. Classes ceased and local ministers of the gospel were sent for. When they came they remained all day leading seekers to faith in Christ. The school was occupied until eleven o'clock that night during which time pupils, teachers, parents and neighbours were convicted and converted. Just one sentence from a penitent youth, anointed by the Spirit of God, and Coleraine was awakened to its spiritual need. Would to God it would happen again.

Repentance by the Ninevites was practical. The sincerity of their repentance was demonstrated and evidenced by the outward expressions they manifested. Besides a change of mind about paganism, they also fasted and put on sackcloth. Fasting is an abstinence from food and legitimate pursuits to permit that more earnest attention be given to spiritual matters.

Some churches today determine major decisions for the church programme according to the state of their bank balance and economic forecasts. The early church reached their decisions after a period of prayer and fasting, "As they ministered to the Lord, and fasted, the Holy Ghost said, Separate me Barnabas and Saul for the work whereunto I have called them. And when they had fasted and prayed, and laid their hands on them, they sent them away" (Acts 13:2), "And when they had ordained them elders in every church, and had prayed with fasting, they commended them to the Lord, on whom they believed" Acts 14:23).

Putting on sackcloth was a token of their sorrow, shame and abasement because of their sins. According to recently discovered records, the Ninevites lived in luxury and opulence which involved the wearing of beautiful garments. With repentance they exchanged the attractive clothing for sackcloth, which was a dark cloth made from the long dark hair of the Oriental goat or camel. As the name suggests, this material was usually used for making sacks, but the Ninevites wore it as a mark of their penitence.

The sincerity of their repentance also demonstrated the inward experience of genuine repentance. True repentance does not treat sin lightly. Besides man and beast being covered in sackcloth, Jonah commanded the Ninevites to "cry mightily unto God: yea, let them turn every one from his evil way, and from the violence that is in their hands." It is one thing to pray about the sins of others, but it is another thing to ask if my hands are clean or if my heart is pure.

Christians who indulge in jealousy, lust, grudges, or broken relationships which they are not prepared to restore, are in danger of coming under the chastening rod of God. From such they need to repent and show evidence of genuine repentance.

Repentance by the Ninevites was powerful. Everyone repented in Nineveh, "from the greatest of them even to the least of them" and "God saw their works, that they turned from their evil way; and God repented of the evil, that he had said that he would do unto them; and he did it not" (Jonah 3:10).

Truly this is a miraculous chapter. It abounds with miracles. There were miracles of repentance; Jonah repented, the people of Nineveh repented, the King of Nineveh repented and finally God repented.

That God should repent begs the questions, "Does God change His mind? Can the unchangeable God change His plans?" We are taught elsewhere in the scriptures that God never changes. He said,

"I am the Lord I change not" (Malachi 3:6). James wrote that there was no variableness in the Father of lights, "neither shadow of turning." I find the words of the Lord to Jeremiah most helpful in this respect, "At what instant I shall speak concerning a nation, and concerning a kingdom, to pluck up, and to pull down, and to destroy it; If that nation, against whom I have pronounced, turn from their evil, I will repent of the evil that I thought to do unto them" (Jeremiah 18:7-8). This throws some light on why judgement was postponed in Nineveh.

God had announced the destruction of Nineveh in forty days, but since the Ninevites had genuinely repented, they stood in a different relationship to God. Upon their repentance God's attitude towards them proved to be different. After his own repentance, the King of Nineveh asked, "Who can tell if God will turn and repent, and turn away from his fierce anger, that we perish not?" (Jonah 3:9).

God is always displeased with evil and ever delights in holiness. It is up to the sinner to make his decision as to whether God will smile or frown on him. According to His promise, God will change His attitude toward the sinner who repents. He will no longer look on the repentant sinner as one who is alienated and under divine wrath, but He will prove to be the welcoming God who is prepared to pardon and justify the sinner. There is therefore no contradiction with God's immutability by God's repenting from His plan to judge. In fact, if God did not repent, it would deny His immutability.

One man who got right with God caused the whole city of Nineveh to repent and come to the Lord. His life, experience and message had been a sign to the Ninevites.

What can one person do in today's society? The experience of Jeremiah Lamphier suggests an answer. He lived in New York during the 1850's when the USA was in a sad state. The crime rate in the city was soaring and widespread violence made the streets unsafe. Immorality and so-called 'free love', which were espoused by many, brought normal family life to the verge of collapse. However, in 1857, Jeremiah Lamphier had a tremendous burden for revival. He called for a handful of believers to meet with him in a location on Fulton

Street, New York, for a prayer meeting to seek God. He arrived at the appointed place on 23 September 1857, where five other earnest Christians joined him. That little meeting gave rise to dozens like it which sprang up all over the United States. Little by little, the divine fires of revival began to spread; hardened sinners were broken, entire Jewish families were saved. The blessings of this revival were not confined to land alone. The crew and passengers on ship after ship arriving in New York Harbour came under deep conviction of sin and were converted.

Those prayer meetings continued and it is estimated that, as a result, over one million people trusted Christ in less than a year. It all began when Jeremiah Lamphier corrected his ways and set out to change his world.

Jeremiah Lamphier and Jonah are testimonies of what God can do and will do through one individual life which is totally yielded to Him.

11 WARTS AND ALL
Jonah 4:1-3

When Oliver Cromwell sat for an official portrait that would portray his appearance to future generations, he was said to have instructed the artist to paint him just as he saw him. Cromwell wanted no flattery to be involved in the painting. The famous Englishman had some disfiguring warts on his face, but he instructed the artist, "Paint me warts and all." Since that time the phrase, "warts and all," has been adopted into the English language as an expression for an unembellished and true representation of a person without covering up any defects.

Jonah concludes this short book that bears his name by revealing a "warts-and-all" picture of himself. I think if I had written this book I might have been tempted to stop at the end of the third chapter for it concludes with a great revival in the city of Nineveh. We all like to have a happy and successful ending.

If this book had ended at the last verse of chapter three, history would have portrayed Jonah as one of the greatest prophets. After all, preaching one message that motivated hundreds of thousands of people to repent and turn to God was no mean accomplishment. However, if we failed to see the real Jonah we would miss many important lessons that this chapter teaches us. God is not impressed by what we try to cover up and hide. The Lord doesn't look on the outward things; He looks at the heart (1 Samuel 16:7) and weighs the motives; "Therefore judge nothing before the time, until the Lord come, who both will bring to light the hidden things of darkness, and will make manifest the counsels of the hearts: and then shall every man have praise of God" (1 Corinthians 4:5).

Chapter four was included in the book because it reveals "the thoughts and intents" of Jonah's heart and exposes his sins. We noted that in the first chapter, Jonah is portrayed as a prodigal prophet insisting on doing his own thing and going his own way just like the New Testament prodigal son of Luke 15. However, in chapter four he is set forth as the prodigal's elder brother; critical, selfish, sullen, angry, and unhappy with the joy that followed his brother's repentance. It is not enough for the servants of the Lord to do the Master's will, we must do "the will of God from the heart" (Ephesians 6:6). At the heart of every problem is the problem of the human heart and that is exactly where Jonah's problems were found.

I know many believers, and especially preachers, who would sacrifice all they have to be able to see the revival which Jonah saw in Nineveh and to be what Jonah was in that city. Yet we read that, "it displeased Jonah exceedingly, and he was very angry" (Jonah 4:1). We would not be surprised if we had read that the pagans and the devil had been upset with this great revival. In the book of Acts, we discover God's blessing incurred the wrath of the ungodly and Christ rejecters. It does surprise us, however, that a true prophet sent by God should become upset with revival which resulted in multitudes of people repenting from their sins.

Jonah was an instrument in the hands of God for a great awakening and was made a channel of blessing to others. Instead of praising God the prophet began to pout; in place of a song Jonah began to sulk; instead of rejoicing Jonah became resentful. However, while it is easy to read of Jonah's resentment we should not close our eyes to the fact that this attitude is neither uncommon nor peculiar to Jonah. One hundred years ago G. Campbell Morgan said, "O brethren, how much of the attitude of Jonah is among us."

I find it amazing that God does not allow Jonah to cover up his displeasure, but rather, lets it all hang out for everyone to read. I see a three-fold perspective in these opening verses: a spiritual perspective, an emotional point of view and an intellectual view.

SPIRITUALLY SPEAKING JONAH STILL HAD HIS PROBLEMS

Geographically Jonah was outside Nineveh; chronologically he was experiencing revival, but spiritually he was almost back to square one.

A few years ago an American psychiatrist wrote a very clever book which became a best seller. In it he postulated three possible stances we may assume in our relationship and interaction with other people. Firstly, I am not okay, but you are. Secondly, I am okay, but you are not. Thirdly, I am okay and you are okay. The first position represents an inferiority complex - I am not okay but you are. The second position indicates a superiority complex - I am okay but you are not. The third position is one without any noticeable complex on either side - I am okay and you are okay.

Most of us have feelings of inferiority and we tend to think that other people do not have the same problems we wrestle with. I am sure you have experienced this in your own life. You might even presume that preachers do not have the doubts you encounter nor do they try to cope with the same habits, weaknesses or failures that you have. Nothing could be further from the truth. Our problem is that we often mask our weaknesses and complexes lest people find out exactly how we feel. We tend to try to project a mature state of grace to those who are seasoned believers.

Have there not been times in your life when you have said, "If only I could experience the power of the Lord in my life like Jonah? I wish I could know the power of the Holy Spirit in my life. I would never have doubts again. I would have no more problems in resisting temptation; it would be victory all the time?"

Let's give some attention to that:

Consider the blessing Jonah witnessed. It is strange that Jonah should be aggrieved that God had granted mercy to the Ninevites when the prophet had also seen God's blessing in his own life. By the mercy of God he had been miraculously preserved in the belly of a fish and had an intimate experience with God. God's grace and mercy had abounded to him in spite of his disobedience and rebellion. We might therefore expect that Jonah would feel he was such a debtor to mercy that he would never have a serious problem in obeying God again. And yet, he did.

Jonah had gone to Nineveh to preach a message of judgement, a message that might have been rejected, but the prophet's message was accepted. Universally the Ninevites repented and God honoured their repentance by granting them mercy. Just as God had been merciful to Jonah, so also mercy was granted to Nineveh and the heavenly fires of revival fell on that city. Although Jonah had freely received mercy from God, yet he had a problem that mercy should also be given to Israel's enemies.

Ponder the bitterness Jonah revealed. The prophet admitted a plain and painful truth about himself when he wrote, "But it displeased Jonah..." (Jonah 4:1). With whom was Jonah so exceedingly displeased? With whom was he very angry? His anger was not directed at the Ninevites. Sad to say, his displeasure was with Jehovah Himself. Jonah showed displeasure because God had not destroyed the city of Nineveh, but instead had chosen to be merciful to repentant sinners.

When God's anger stopped, Jonah's anger started. The word "angry" which is used here conveys the sense "to burn with anger." Jonah was burning with rage. He was furious and fuming. That is exactly what resentment does. Resentment leads to bitterness which destroys our joy and peace.

An evidence that a person is really filled with the Spirit of God is that he displays the fruit of the Spirit which is "love, joy, peace, longsuffering, gentleness, goodness, faith, meekness, temperance: against such there is no law" (Galatians 5:22-23). Jonah could not hide this prominent flaw, a 'wart', which was a spirit of resentment and anger. So bad was his resentment that he went outside the city. He sat down with his heart still filled with bitterness and prayed, "Lord take my life from me."

Does this not remind you again of the prodigal's elder brother in the fifteenth chapter of Luke? Of him we read that "he was angry and would not go in (to the feast)" (Luke 15:28). A further parallel to this is that the elder brother was not irritated with his brother as much as he was with his father. This anger was prompted because his prodigal brother was receiving so much attention and he was not.

Unhappily we recognise that this spirit of bitterness is still abroad today among some Christians who manifest the same attitude toward their Heavenly Father. Some become angry at God because He appears to favour some believers with greater blessings than they themselves are experiencing. Even among pastors, evangelists and missionaries there are some who become angry with God because some other worker is seemingly being blessed in a greater way than they are.

Be vigilant not to fall into the trap of thinking that because God blesses you or blesses others through you, that you have arrived and have reached a higher plain than other Christians. Remember that men at best are only men and no one is above problems. Like Jonah, Elijah was another famous prophet. It was after he saw the fire of God fall on Mount Carmel and took part in the destruction of the false prophets of Baal that he encountered the greatest struggle of his life. Under a Juniper tree he sat down and complained, "It is enough, now O Lord, take away my life" (1 Kings 19:4). Scottish preacher, Robert Murray McCheyne, said on one occasion, "I find in my heart the seeds of every known sin."

EMOTIONALLY SPEAKING JONAH STILL HAD HIS PAST

To some extent Jonah's past overshadowed and influenced his present. Notice the contrast between God's response to Nineveh's repentance and Jonah's response to it. When God saw that the city of Nineveh repented He had compassion, "And God saw their works, that they turned from their evil way; and God repented of the evil, that he had said that he would do unto them; and he did it not..." In his prayer Jonah complained, "I knew that thou art a gracious God, and merciful, slow to anger, and of great kindness, and repentest thee of the evil" (Jonah 3:10-4:2).

When Jonah saw God's response to the Ninevites' repentance he was aggrieved and depressed, "But it displeased Jonah exceedingly, and he was very angry" (Jonah 4:1). I think this tells us something of the character of Jonah in contrast to the character of God. Jonah became very angry, whereas God is "slow to anger".

Why should Jonah have been so upset about God having compassion on the Ninevites? Different people have given various reasons for Jonah's attitude. The variant opinions suggest that the prophet's attitude is not easily understood. Personally, I think his demeanor and approach insinuate two things about Jonah:

Revival in Nineveh threatened Jonah's prestige as a prophet. It was as if the pouting prophet was saying, "If I can't have my way, I don't want to live." Here is a man of God and a servant of God down in the dumps. His pride was hurt because he felt that his ministry had been discredited.

Moses wrote about the following about a prophet; "When a prophet speaketh in the name of the Lord, if the thing follow not, nor come to pass, that is the thing which the Lord hath not spoken, but the prophet hath spoken it presumptuously: thou shalt not be afraid of him" (Deuteronomy 18:22). Jonah felt his ministry had been discredited and his prophetic pronouncement of judgement did not come to pass. The prophet had spoken in the name of the Lord; he had cried against Nineveh of impending judgement, "Yet forty days and Nineveh will be overthrown" (Jonah 3:4), but that judgement did not happen.

It is interesting that after making his declaration of imminent doom, "Jonah went out of the city" to nurse his wounded spirit. If ever there was a time Jonah needed to be in the city it was during the days that followed the great turning to God. The thousands who had repented were in need of a prophet's guidance, teaching and shepherding, but Jonah left town, abandoned them and left them as sheep without a shepherd. Now we meet him sitting outside the city, half hoping Nineveh would fall so he could say, "I told you so."

Resentment is basically self-centredness, which is sin. Being displeased with God is always an evidence of selfishness. The basic cause of that displeasure is that we while we want God's will, we would rather have it in our way. To do God's will is to deny our will and delight in His will. Jesus said, "If any man will come after me, let him deny himself, and take up his cross, and follow me" (Matthew 16:24). We are either committed to self-will or God's will.

Further evidence of Jonah's selfishness is betrayed by his use of ten personal pronouns as he addressed God in prayer. "He prayed...I...my...I...my...I...I...I...my...me...me" (Jonah 2, 3). Jonah's prayer was egocentric and, generally, egocentric people cannot hide their selfishness.

Too many Christians have selfishly "gone out of the city" when they should have gone into the highways and byways compelling the lost to come to Christ. Some abandon the city to escape the burdens and heartaches that people are carrying. Instead of abandoning the needy we need to be near to them and put an arm around them to show that we care.

As a prophet Jonah wanted personal vindication of his own prophecy. What Jonah wanted was to go to the edge of the city and watch Nineveh burn. Perhaps one or two people might have come along to say, "Jonah you were right." To this Jonah might have said, "I told you so." However, that did not happen and because it didn't, Jonah was angry.

Could Jonah have therefore thought to himself, *What of my reputation as a prophet in Israel? What of my reputation in Nineveh? Surely my reputation is in ruins?* Jonah was too concerned about his own reputation, not only before the Ninevites, but before the Jews back home.

This is a good time to ask what concerns you most. Are you more interested in reputation than character? Reputation is what people think we are, character is what God **knows** we are. Evangelist D.L. Moody said that character is "what a man is in the dark."

We must be willing to die to our own reputation and prestige so that our greatest motivation for Christian service is God's glory. That is exactly what our Saviour did for "He made Himself of no reputation" (Philippians 2:6). Paul tells us that the same mind of Christ should dwell, or be at home, in us.

Revival in Nineveh threatened Jonah's prejudice as a patriot. Jonah loved his country. In Jonah 4:2 he spoke of Israel as "my country". Jonah was a Jew through and through and the very idea that the Gentile nations, especially wicked Nineveh, were to experience mercy and pardon from God was repugnant to him. Jonah hated those Gentile dogs, nor could he accept that God would visit non-Jewish nations with blessing.

Forgive me, but sometimes I can identify with how Jonah must have felt. The more I travel in this world the more I love to come home to our "wee province" of Ulster, Northern Ireland. In spite of the problems in our society, God has blessed us in so many ways. The problem arises, however, when we view another country as not included in the offer of God's grace. This becomes a prejudice that ceases to reflect the heart of Christ. We need to be careful that we are not so biased against those who do not belong to our denominational group that we cannot rejoice with them when God blesses them.

I heard the story of two churches in one of the Southern States of USA. One of the churches was a Baptist and the other was a Methodist and they were just across the street from each other. Instead of displaying respect and Christian love, there was great rivalry between the two congregations. The Baptists distained the Methodist Arminian teaching emphasising their doctrine that "once saved always saved." The Methodists were equally avid in their defense of their position replying, "It is possible to lose your salvation." Both of these churches organised evangelistic revivals in their respective churches. On one occasion the Methodist Church and the Baptist Church conducted twelve days of such meetings at the same time. When the series of meetings finished one Baptist was heard to say, "Well, we didn't have much of a revival, but thank God the Methodists didn't have much of a revival either." Now that is prejudice.

Do we become envious when God blesses others or do we rejoice wherever and whenever God chooses to bless?

INTELLECTUALLY SPEAKING JONAH STILL HAD HIS PROPOSITION

Attempting to reason things out for himself, Jonah offered some suggestions to God. What were these suggestions? Jonah 4:2 gives us an insight into the prophet's reasoning, "And he prayed unto the Lord, and said, I pray thee, O Lord, was not this my saying, when I was yet in my country? Therefore I fled before unto Tarshish: for I knew that thou art a gracious God, and merciful, slow to anger, and of great kindness, and repentest thee of the evil." It is clear that Jonah was preaching in his prayer. It is sad when a believer uses the public prayer meeting as an opportunity to direct his point of view to fellow-believers. When we pray we should be talking exclusively to God. However, in his prayer Jonah was reasoning that God truly is gracious, merciful, patient, kind and forgiving. That implies that Jonah's affirmations about God were correct, but his conclusions were all wrong.

Jonah's doctrine was all right. There was nothing wrong with Jonah's theology. He knew God was the God of grace who freely bestows His undeserved favour to hell-deserving sinners. This theology concurs with what Paul wrote to Titus, "For we ourselves also were sometimes foolish, disobedient, deceived, serving divers lusts and pleasures, living in malice and envy, hateful, and hating one another. But after that the kindness and love of God our Saviour toward man appeared" (Titus 3:3-4).

Jonah understood what it meant that God should be merciful. Mercy is the opposite of justice. Mercy spares from that which we do deserve. A man who was having his photograph taken asked the photographer, "Will it do me justice?"

The photographer looked at the man again and with a twinkle in his eye said, "Justice? Sir, it is not justice you need, it is mercy."

If God dealt with us as justice demands then we would all be in hell. But God is a God of mercy. In his great Psalm of praise King David said, "He hath not dealt with us after our sins; nor rewarded us according to our iniquities. For as the heaven is high above the earth, so great is his mercy toward them that fear him. As far as the east is from the west, so far hath he removed our transgressions from us" (Psalm 103:10-12). The Lord is great and greatly to be praised. He not only sustains His universe moment by moment, but He also has time to listen to the sinner who cries to Him in repentance.

On examination of Jonah's prayer we see that he had a proper view of God and His attributes.

Jonah's deduction was all wrong. Although Jonah was perfectly orthodox and fundamental in the doctrine of God, yet he drew the wrong conclusions from that doctrine. Jonah reasoned that since God so easily forgives sin and pardons sinners, it did not really matter whether he lived or laboured for God. In other words, Jonah concluded that such a merciful and forgiving God would excuse the prophet's disobedience because the Lord was not dependent on a human instrument like Jonah, a Galilean preacher, to do His work.

Paul dealt with these same issues of Christian life and labour in his letter to the Romans. After expounding the great doctrine of justification by faith alone in Christ alone in Romans 5, Paul anticipated someone asking, "Shall we continue in sin that grace may abound?" (Romans 6:1). In Romans chapters 6 & 7 Paul provides us with an answer to that question. He stressed how important it was to yield our lives as instruments of righteousness and live for God. In Romans chapter 8 & 9 Paul introduced the doctrine of election and expected someone to ask, "If believers are elected and foreordained then why preach the gospel?" In Romans 10 Paul explained that a preacher is necessary to communicate the gospel because sinners cannot call on the Lord if they have not believed on Him, and they cannot believe in Him if they have not heard of Him, nor can they hear of Him without a preacher, nor can the messenger preach except he is sent. Paul concluded, "Faith cometh by hearing, and hearing by the word of God" (Romans 10:17). Paul admonished his readers to live obediently and labour continually for God.

Jonah's conclusions led him to think that he was superfluous to God's plan and was no longer needed. For that reason in his prayer he asked to die, "Lord take my life from me" (Jonah 4:3). Jonah forgot that God does need us, He includes us. He has been pleased to choose us and has ordained that through the foolishness of preaching sinners might believe. Preaching is still God's primary means for evangelisation.

Perhaps you feel that you are not needed in God's work. You look at your talents, or lack of them, and think of them in light of your failures, or even reckon you are too old. None of these reasons disqualify us from God's service. He still needs you and me. The Lord is worth living for and labouring for.

It would be a terrible thing to know all the truth about God and keep it to ourselves. Our God is such a wonderful God that we should worship Him! Trust Him! Glorify Him! Preach Him to all and extol Him high. Charles Wesley expressed well when he wrote:

Jesus the name high over all,
In hell, or earth, or sky:
Angels and men before it fall,
And devils fear and fly.

Happy, if with my latest breath
I might but gasp His name:
Preach Him to all, and cry in death
Behold, behold the Lamb!

12 OUR WONDERFUL GOD
Jonah 4:1-11

Jonah's traumatic journey might have been entitled, *"The Missionary Experience."* The prophet was taken out of his normal home environment, made to work under pressures that neither he nor any one else had ever before experienced. He suffered all the frustrations any missionary might meet in coping with a new culture and a foreign language. The accumulation of these things are enough to bring out the very worst in the most restrained person and they often they do. There is nothing like stress to bring hitherto unknown or dormant sensitivities to the surface. When this happens it can disrupt harmony in a mission situation, the unity of a church fellowship or peace in a home.

New missionaries might arrive in a country of God's calling like bold knights riding into the arena of conflict. With high aspirations and expectations for fervent evangelism and church planting they throw themselves into the work only to suffer a setback at the early hurdles. Such workers may not be aware that God has possibly moved them to another part of the world as much for his own sanctification as for that of others.

Here was Jonah in a foreign country with a hostile atmosphere, experiencing a different culture and different climate. Although far from home, the prophet had not abandoned his narrow-minded prejudice against the Ninevites. He carried with him an air of conceited pride that he was an Israelite and not a Gentile dog. One missionary testified of a similar attitude on arriving on his field of service when he admitted, "I never knew what a heart of stone I had until I went overseas."

In recent years it has been my privilege to minister the Word of God in other lands and I have discovered the same attitude arising in my own heart. I have had to learn some lessons about other cultures and people whose ways are alien to ours. Such trips and experiences have been as much as for my own good, as for the good of those to whom I went to minister.

The Lord eventually brought Jonah to Nineveh, not only that he might be a channel of blessing to others, but that God might purge and eliminate his narrow-mindedness and bias. We might ask if it worked. It seems that the lesson must have got through to Jonah for he wrote these four chapters in which he exposed his own prejudices as an admission of error.

By Jonah giving us this journal of his time in Nineveh he was admitting that instead of praising God for revival as he should have, he had indulged his time in pouting and prejudice. Instead of singing praises, he was sulking in self-pity; instead of rejoicing in the salvation of the lost, he resented that his plans and opinions were ignored. Jonah was angry because his prophecy was not vindicated and God did not destroy Nineveh. As a result of this anger he prayed, "Lord, take my life from me" (Jonah 4:3). It is a good thing that the Lord does not always answer our prayers the way we want. Such a thing happened to Moses when he asked God to allow him to enter Canaan, the Promised Land. God answered him, "But the Lord was wroth with me for your sakes, and would not hear me: and the Lord said unto me, Let it suffice thee; speak no more unto me of this matter" (Deuteronomy 3:26).

Indeed, instead of taking Jonah at his word, the Lord graciously asked him, "Doest thou well to be angry?" Here again God revealed just how wonderful He is. Indeed, in each chapter of this prophecy something "*great*" about God is portrayed. In chapter 1 God was responsible for sending the *great storm*. In chapter 2 God sent the *great fish*. In chapter 3 God sent a *great revival* to the *great city* of Nineveh. Now, in chapter four Jonah majored on the greatest truth of all, the revelation of the *great God of heaven*. Campbell Morgan said, "So many have focused on the great fish that they have forgotten the great God."

Jonah's prophecy is not primarily about Jonah, or the storm, or the fish, or Nineveh. It is a revelation of God. God is mentioned 38 times in these four short chapters, whereas Jonah's name is mentioned fewer than half of that number. If we were to eliminate God from the four chapters, the story would not make sense.

This is a prophecy about the providence of God. What is providence? Perhaps the best definition was provided by theologian Louis Berkhof when he wrote, "Providence is that work of God in which He preserves all His creatures, is active in all that happens in the world, and directs all things to their appointed end."

We have a wonderful God whose works are as wondrous as His person.

GOD'S WONDERFUL PATIENCE WITH JONAH

We frequently speak of the patience of Job, but have you ever considered the patience of God? God's patience is a quality we often overlook. Paul made reference to it when he wrote to the Romans, "Now the God of patience and consolation grant you to be likeminded one toward another according to Christ Jesus" (Romans 15:5). Patience is a lovely quality.

At the beginning of the Revelation of Jesus Christ which was given to the apostle John while he was imprisoned on the Isle of Patmos, he wrote, "I John, who also am your brother, and companion in tribulation, and in the kingdom and patience of Jesus Christ was in the isle that is called Patmos, for the word of God, and for the testimony of Jesus Christ" (Revelation 1:9). The quality that John needed as he suffered for the Kingdom was exactly that which he displayed while under pressure.

You and I can become so impatient; impatient with God, impatient under temptation and trial, impatient with one another and even impatient with ourselves. However, God is patient. He is "slow to anger and plenteous in mercy" (Jonah 4:2).

God was patient with Jonah's activity. God had every reason to reject Jonah and look for another. He might well have done so when Jonah first fled to Tarshish. "But the Lord sent out a great wind" (Jonah 1:4).

The Lord could have cast him aside when Jonah went "down into the sides of the ship" (Jonah 1:5) to escape from the storm. But God had a way of overruling the sailors' decision when they drew lots and Jonah was indicated.

When Jonah was thrown overboard God had opportunity to let him drown, but the Lord prepared a great fish to swallow the disobedient prophet. God not only preserved His servant in the bowels of the fish but also gave him a second chance, "And the word of the Lord came unto Jonah the second time" (Jonah 3:1).

After so much mercy and longsuffering from God we might think that Jonah would have learned his lesson. Do you not think that if a man had survived three days and three nights in the belly of a fish, repented and was glad to discover that God still loved him and cared for him, he would surely learn to not grieve God again?

We may look at Jonah as a distant character who lived several millennia ago. However, some of Jonah's traits still exist with us today. This prophet was no different from you and me. Commentator Warren Wiersbe says, "It took God longer to prepare His servant and get him to obey His call than it did for the entire godless city of Nineveh to repent."

Things have not changed much. It is a shameful indictment on Christians that it still takes longer for believers to repent and get right with God than for the unconverted to repent and come to Christ. Most of us would have thrown the disobedient Jonah out of our churches a long time ago. Are you not glad that He is the God of patience? He was patient with Jonah and He is patient with us.

Have you not discovered this to be so in your own spiritual experience? How many times might God have ditched us because of our recurring failures? Perhaps there have been many times when you might have given up on yourself only to find that God had not given up on you. The Lord has stayed with you through those frustrating days. He cared, guided and protected you through succeeding years. From personal experience we can all say, "The Lord is gracious, and full of compassion; slow to anger and of great mercy" (Psalm 145:8).

God was patient with Jonah's audacity. When God saw how the Ninevites repented, fasted and covered themselves and their animals with sackcloth, He had compassion on them. When Jonah saw God's compassion for the ungodly Gentiles he was displeased. God also saw Jonah's anger and confronted him, "Do you do well to be angry?" (Jonah 4:4). Did Jonah any grounds to be angry with God or to question the ways and purposes of God? Jesus asked His critics, "Is it not lawful for me to do what I will with mine own? Is thine eye evil, because I am good?" (Matthew 20:15). In his Commentary on Jonah, Faber wrote, "Losing our temper with God is a more common thing in the spiritual life than many suppose."

Do you become angry with God? Perhaps you have been bitter and resentful with the Lord because of the way some circumstances have transpired. The Lord has reason to ask, "Do you do well to be angry?"

I find it interesting how God counselled Jonah. Here is the picture of the Divine Parent dealing with His wayward, angry and sulking child. God did not condone Jonah's attitude, nor did He condemn Jonah. Rather, He understood and sympathised with the downcast prophet.

There are three recognised ways of counselling people. God could have said, "Jonah, you are right to be angry and get it out of your system." Some people might suggest that this would have been the right reply.

The Lord could have also said, "You are wrong to be angry." This reply would have undoubtedly made Jonah feel guilty.

However, God did not condone or condemn His child. He simply asked, "Do you do well to be angry?" In fact, the statement can be translated from the Hebrew as "You are angry, aren't you?" God manifested His concern for the prophet. Perhaps the best way for parents to react to enraged children is to say, "You're angry, aren't you?" Such a reply conveys a sense of understanding and concern. It was in this masterly way that God dealt with Jonah.

He is the God of patience who understood Jonah and understands you and me. How many times have you questioned the Lord's ways, His purpose and providences? The Lord has listened to our complaints and instead of condemning us, He is sympathetic and understanding. Martha and Mary blamed the Lord Jesus for delaying two days during which time their brother Lazarus died. Mary said, "Lord if Thou hadst been here, my brother had not died" (John 11:32). The sisters were obviously irritated that Jesus did not come sooner. They felt that their Lord had let them down. The Saviour did not reprimand their complaints. Instead, when they were grieved, He was grieved; when they wept, He wept. He understood their hurt and disappointment.

When we feel that no one cares, Jesus is there to weep with us. The Saviour understands our hurts and cares for us.

GOD'S PROVISION FOR JONAH

The depressed and frustrated prophet went outside the city, gathered together a few twigs and branches to make himself a makeshift tent to give protection from the sun's bright and scorching rays. Nothing is hidden from the Lord and He saw the situation. The Lord had already been gracious to Jonah and now showed further compassion on the dejected prophet, "And the Lord God prepared a gourd, and made it to come up over Jonah, that it might be a shadow over his head, to deliver him from his grief. So Jonah was exceeding glad of the gourd" (Jonah 4:6).

This was another token of God's provision. In an earlier chapter we noticed that God prepared "a great fish". Now, "God prepared a gourd," He subsequently prepared "a worm" (Jonah 4:7) and finally "God prepared a vehement east wind" (Jonah 4:8).

Some translators speak of the gourd as a vine. Others are more specific and think it was a castor oil plant. Perhaps it is unkind to say that castor oil was appropriate for Jonah needed a good dose of it. In all probability the gourd was a fast-growing perennial plant which reached a height of some 8 - 10 feet and looked similar to a palm tree with large overhanging leaves.

The gourd was provided specifically for Jonah's need. The patient and merciful God of heaven sent the gourd to Jonah with a kind design. "It to come up over Jonah, that it might be a shadow over his head, to deliver him from his grief. So Jonah was exceeding glad of the gourd" (Jonah 4:6). Someone has said that this was God's way of cooling down His hotheaded servant. How gracious of God to care for his pouting prophet.

The Psalmist stresses that our Heavenly Father always knows our frame and remembers that we are dust. He ministers to us in our physical needs. Imagine Jonah waking that morning and seeing this beautiful palm-like plant inviting him to sit under its shadow. He might have said, "Well this is more like it, I knew the Lord was with me after all." Jonah obviously took the gourd as a sign that God was with him. However, the plant was only as a temporary providence to comfort Jonah.

We are all guilty of rejoicing in our temporary blessings more than those of eternal value. Like Jonah, we also are glad of the comfort-giving gourds, our earthly comforts and temporal luxuries.

The gourd was transitory in its nature. God is not only the author of eternal blessing, but His mercies are also new every morning. For Jonah He not only prepared a gourd, "But God prepared a worm when the morning rose the next day, and it smote the gourd that it withered" (Jonah 4:7). The Lord gave the gourd and then removed it.

The same God who measures our discouragement also knows our encouragements. Jonah had enjoyed the benefit of the sheltering gourd for one day during which he really appreciated it as a token from God. How did Jonah react when he lost that which he had cherished? He lamented his loss, "And it came to pass, when the sun did arise, that God prepared a vehement east wind; and the sun beat upon the head of Jonah, that he fainted, and wished in himself to die, and said, It is better for me to die than to live" (Jonah 4:8).

Often God has to force open our fingers when we cling to those things we mistakenly cherish to our own detriment. God wanted Jonah to rejoice in Him and not in the gourd. Our supreme ground for comfort must not be the changing circumstances of life, but in the unchanging God of heaven.

We must learn to trust the Lord when we cannot sense His presence, when our prayers remain unanswered or when our families still continue unmoved and unconverted. Earlier the Lord had said to Jonah, "Do you do well to be angry?" God now probes a little deeper, "Do you do well to be angry about the gourd?" (Jonah 4:9).

Jeannette George was the lady who played the role of Corrie Ten Boom in the film, "The Hiding Place." In the film Corrie spoke of the wonderful times of fellowship she had in the Ravensbruck Concentration Camp with her sister Betsy before her death. Corrie Ten Boom, along with her father and her sister Betsy, had hidden Jews from the Nazis above their clock shop in Rotterdam. Their secret labour of love was discovered and consequently the three were sent to a Nazi concentration camp.

The girls were sent to Ravensbruck and never saw their father again. The long days of horrible suffering resulted in Corrie's heart hardening with resentment toward God and bitterness filling her life. However, through her radiant countenance and her caring conversations, Betsy spread the love of the Lord throughout the camp. When Betsy died in the Nazi concentration camp, Corrie heard the Lord ask her, "Do you have a right to be angry about the gourd?" Corrie was broken. She yielded to her Lord and avowed to serve Him all her days.

Upon her release at the end of the war Corrie picked up Betsy's mantle and spread the message of Christ's love throughout the world. Corrie Ten Boom is in heaven today, but she left us the legacy of her testimony in the film, "The Hiding Place," and many other books in which she told of God's patience, God's protection and God's pardon in her life.

When we are more taken up with the blessings instead of the Blesser, God often sends worms to remove our gourd. Do we have a right to be angry when God removes the gourds of our lives? Thank God for the gourd, but also learn to thank Him for the worm when God takes away the things we cherish.

That was the painful lesson that Job learned many years earlier when he finally said, "The Lord gave, and the Lord has taken away; blessed be the Name of the Lord" (Job 1:21).

GOD'S PITY IN JONAH

Would it have been possible that Jonah might have repented from his stubborn opposition and prejudice against the universality of God's grace? Did Jonah really learn his lesson? I think we can affirm that he did. By writing this book he admitted his error and let God have the last word in evaluating his life.

Jonah saw his actions and attitude were obnoxious in the eyes of God. When believers put things before people it is abhorrent before God. God has designed that we love people and use things, but we live in times when people love things and use people.

The Lord began to reason with Jonah from the lesser to the greater, "And God said to Jonah, Doest thou well to be angry for the gourd? And he said, I do well to be angry, even unto death. Then said the Lord, Thou hast had pity on the gourd, for the which thou hast not laboured, neither madest it grow; which came up in a night, and perished in a night: And should not I spare Nineveh, that great city, wherein are more than sixscore thousand persons that cannot discern between their right hand and their left hand; and also much cattle?" (Jonah 4:9-11).

There was a stark contrast between Jonah and God. Jonah was concerned about a plant, whereas God was concerned about a people. Jonah was concerned over something for which he had not laboured. God was concerned over His creation. Jonah was concerned about something which is temporal. God was concerned about souls which are eternal. Paul reminded the Corinthians, "While we look not at the things which are seen, but at the things which are not seen: for the things which are seen are temporal; but the things which are not seen are eternal" (2 Corinthians 4:18).

We can tell a lot about people by observing what it is that makes them happy and what makes them sad. Some Christians rejoice superficially when others are saved, but they rejoice greatly when their own personal needs are met. Jonah was more happy about his vine than he was about revival. God still has got a store of worms which He can send to consume and remove those things that blur our view of eternal values.

Jonah saw what was precious in the eyes of God. The psalmist said, "Precious in the sight of the Lord is the death of His saints" (Psalm 116:15). We may safely conclude from the closing verse in Jonah that, "Precious in the eyes of the Lord are the souls of His creatures."

Here are a several things that are precious in the eyes of the Lord:

Souls are precious to God. God said, "Should not I spare Nineveh, that great city, wherein are more than sixscore thousand persons that cannot discern between their right hand and their left hand; and also much cattle?" (Jonah 4:11). Jonah was a pitiful spectacle, giving more value to the temporal plant than to the needy population of Nineveh. Sadly, some of us are so like him. May God help us to look at our world through the Saviour's eyes.

Souls in great cities are precious to God. "Should I not spare Nineveh, that great city". It was estimated that Nineveh's population was over one million people. The challenge of reaching the multitudes has assumed gigantic proportions in our day. Six billion people populate our world and the Lord still asks, "Whom shall I send and who will go for us?" (Isaiah 6:8).

Can you answer, "Here am I send me?"

Souls in great cities that cannot discern between their right hand and their left hand are precious to God. Undoubtedly this refers to little children who were too young to know the difference between right and wrong.

Thank God for those who are engaged in the evangelisation of children. It is a work that is very close to the heart of God. Well do we sing, "Jesus loves the little children, all the children of the world."

Our Lord Jesus looked over the panorama of Jerusalem and wept over the city, "And when He was come near, He beheld the city, and wept over it" (Luke 19:41). God not only had pity on the great city, but also on the boys and girls of those cities. "Jesus said, Suffer little children, and forbid them not, to come unto me: for of such is the kingdom of heaven" (Matthew 19:14).

People ask why God does not come down and put the world right. One day He will. Jesus will come with His saints to judge the nations and establish His Millennial Reign. In the meantime, God is patient and so long-suffering. In his day, Peter answered those who asked why God delayed His coming, "The Lord is not slack concerning his promise, as some men count slackness; but is longsuffering to us-ward, not willing that any should perish, but that all should come to repentance" (2 Peter 3:9).

Martin Luther once said, "If I had been God I would have kicked the whole rotten world to pieces long ago." We probably would have done the same, but our God is compassionate.

This four-chapter prophecy ends with Jonah being stunned to silence. His mouth was stopped and he had no reply to God. There was neither agreement nor disapproval, and certainly there was no repentance from his stubborn pouting because God had granted mercy to Nineveh.

All of Jonah's experience is a mirror which reflects our own experience with God. We have all experienced times when it has been difficult to surrender to God's will. The bitter flow of prejudice, anger and resentment towards other people has also surfaced in our hearts. Our hearts have been laid bare but the sovereign God who showed mercy to Nineveh also accords mercy and grace to us in our times of need.

May the Lord help us to learn from Jonah's failures and be blessed by God's faithfulness. His mercy greets us every morning and every day brings new tokens of His loving kindness to us.

The prophecy of Jonah is reckoned to be about two and a half thousand years old. However, antiquity has not robbed this book of its relevance in the twenty-first century. The sovereign God who dispenses mercy and grace is still at work in our world today.

Just this week I met our brother Fu Teng (not his real name) from Vietnam. Fu was born in Hanoi and lived through the latter days of the heavy bombing of the Vietnamese capital at the end of the War. Those terrifying bombs only reinforced Fu's parents' entrenched commitment to the communist cause in their homeland.

Fu was an intelligent and hard working student who rose up through the ranks until he earned himself a secure position in a state run business with many workers subordinate to him. However, despite his successful career, he felt that his life was empty. During this time he thought that if he could only get out of Vietnam there might be better possibilities for him.

When he heard of other discontents leaving Vietnam on homemade vessels he decided to follow them. He gathered what money and belongings he had, which he pooled with other funds to pay for a homemade boat. He hoped the trip would not only take him and the other refugees away from Vietnam, but also possibly open the door to a better life and achieve his goal of security and prosperity.

It was a daring venture for him and his fellow escapees when they pushed off from the shores of their homeland and said their final farewell to Vietnam. The fragile vessel made little headway as it floated almost aimlessly day after day on the calm swell of the China Sea. It is difficult for an atheistic communist to pray, but as the boat people lazily drifted along the ocean currents, they became very fearful for their survival as rations began to run low without any sign of land or a passing ship.

Finally, after twenty-six days of wayward drifting, the small group of impoverished and starving refugees were picked up by a passing merchant ship and taken to Hong Kong. Instead of the realisation of their dreams for freedom and prosperity, the refugees were imprisoned with thousands of other refugees from Vietnam in a specially prepared detention camp. Fu was shattered. He had landed in prison and was much worse off than he had ever been in his whole life. Not only had he not reached his hopeful destination, he had lost everything he ever owned, including a position of influence in the communist regime. He could not help but rue leaving his homeland and pondered, *If only I had not fled Vietnam.*

At the detention centre Fu diligently applied himself to studying English as well as teaching Vietnamese children. Although he had turned his back on Vietnam, he was still an avowed communist and atheist. He had not known any other life. As a teacher and respected leader in the camp, he tried to impart his communist virtues to the children in his class.

One day some Americans visited the camp to help the children with their English. Fu decided to stay in the class and listen to the foreigners. He stood at the back of the class and listened intently, trying to improve his English vocabulary. He was not aware that these visitors were missionaries for they didn't carry a Bible. Fu was so prejudiced against God and the gospel that if he had seen a Bible he certainly would have left the class immediately.

The visitors spoke with simple and plain English in which they told a story that Fu had never heard before. They spoke about a Shepherd who owned a hundred sheep, but one night he lost one. Fu was captivated and listened attentively as the friends told how this Shepherd not only knew every sheep, but loved them all to the extent that He was prepared to leave the ninety and nine sheep in the safety of the sheep pen while He went to look for the one that was lost. When He eventually found the lost sheep, the poor and pitiful animal was in grave danger and at the point of death. Mercifully, the Shepherd arrived in the nick of time and rescued the helpless sheep. The kind Shepherd sympathetically carried his sheep back to the fold on His strong shoulders and was so happy that He called all the family together to celebrate the great rescue.

Fu was mesmerised by the story and felt it was one of the best he had ever heard. As a teacher he decided to ask the visitors to tell the story again, but just then a lady started to strum her guitar and sing. Fu was sure she was singing a romantic ballad as her sweet voice matched her sparkling smile as she sang, "He is my everything, He is my all. He is my everything, both great and small. He gave His life for me, made everything new, He is my everything, now how about you?"

Fu was sure this lady was singing of her boyfriend or husband. It was only later that he realised that the Shepherd in the story and the One of whom the lady sang was Jesus. Fu's heart was touched and his conscience was smitten. After he heard the gospel he could not sleep and only found peace when he repented from his sin and believed on the Saviour with all his heart.

Until that time Fu had never heard of Jesus nor the gospel, but when Christ entered his heart, his life was transformed.

The long time spent at the detention camp might have seemed worse than the long days drifting at sea, had it not been that Fu was able to invest this time to learn more and more about the Lord Jesus, the Bible and his obligations as a Christian. It was during this time that Fu had a complete change of heart and opinion about Vietnam. Just when he felt he was able to get away from it forever, he felt God was asking him to go back to Hanoi and preach the gospel to his fellow countrymen. At first he resisted God's call. There was the possibility of a new life in the West. God was at work in his life and Fu came to the realisation that if the Lord had been merciful to him, how could he deny mercy to those who still lived under the heel of communist tyranny? He finally yielded to the will of God and was glad to return to the Vietnamese capital.

Today Fu is a pastor and evangelist among his own people. Because of his obedience Fu has had the joy of leading thousands of his friends and neighbours to Jesus Christ, including his parents and many of his own family circle. Think of what might have happened if Fu had refused to go back to the place that he had first fled from.

The sovereign God of heaven showed mercy to Fu that he might in turn be an instrument of mercy to Vietnam.

The God of Jonah still lives today.